S0-BIY-862

THE PLAIN DEALER

by William Wycherley

A programme/text with commentary by Simon Trussler

Contents

Swan Theatre Plays published by Methuen London
by arrangement with the Royal Shakespeare Company

The Royal Shakespeare Company (RSC), is the title under which the Royal Shakespeare Theatre, Stratford-upon-Avon, has operated since 1961. Now one of the best-known theatre companies in the world, the RSC builds on a long and distinguished history of theatre in Stratford-upon-Avon.

In essence, the aim of the Company is the same as that expressed in 1905 by Sir Frank Benson, then director of the Stratford theatre: 'to train a company, every member of which would be an essential part of a homogeneous whole, consecrated to the practice of the dramatic arts and especially to the representation of the plays of Shakespeare'. The RSC is formed around a core of associate artists – actors, directors, designers and others – with the aim that their different skills should combine, over the years, to produce a distinctive approach to theatre, both classical and modern.

When, just a year after the granting, in 1925, of its Royal Charter, the theatre was almost completely destroyed by fire, a worldwide campaign was launched to build a new one. Productions moved to a local cinema until the new theatre, designed by Elisabeth Scott, was opened by the Prince of Wales on 23 April, 1932. Over the next thirty years, under the influence of directors such as Robert Atkins, Bridges-Adams, Iden Payne, Komisarjevsky, Sir Barry Jackson, Glen Byam Shaw and Anthony Quayle, the Shakespeare Memorial Theatre maintained a worldwide reputation.

In 1960, the newly appointed artistic director, Peter Hall, extended the re-named Royal Shakespeare Company's operations to include a London base at the Aldwych Theatre, and widened the Company's repertoire to include modern as well as classical work. Other innovations of the period which have shaped today's Company were the travelling Theatre-go-round and experimental work which included the Theatre of Cruelty season.

Under Trevor Nunn, who took over as artistic director in 1968, this experimental work in small performance spaces led, in 1974, to the opening of The Other Place, Stratford-upon-Avon. This was a rehearsal space converted into a theatre and in 1977 its London counterpart, The Warehouse, opened with a policy of presenting new British plays. In the same year the RSC played its first season in Newcastle upon Tyne – now an annual event. In 1978, the year in which Terry Hands joined Trevor Nunn as artistic director, the RSC also fulfilled an ambition to tour towns and villages with little or no access to live professional theatre.

In 1982, the RSC moved its London base to the Barbican Centre in the City of London, opening both the Barbican Theatre, specially built for the RSC by the generosity of the Corporation of the City of London, and The Pit, a small theatre converted like The Warehouse and The Other Place, from a rehearsal room.

The 1986 season saw the opening of this new RSC theatre: the Swan. Built within the section of the shell of the original Shakespeare Memorial Theatre which escaped the 1926 fire, the Swan is a Jacobean-style playhouse staging the once hugely popular but now rarely-seen plays of Shakespeare's contemporaries during the period 1570-1750. This new dimension to the Royal Shakespeare Company's work has been made possible by the extremely generous gift of Frederick R. Koch, the RSC's benefactor. In 1987 the RSC, supported by Frank and Woji Gero and Playhouse Productions, and by Eddie Kulukundis, presented a season at the Mermaid Theatre, London, which included the Swan repertoire and two American plays. In early 1987 Terry Hands became sole Artistic Director and Chief Executive of the Company.

Throughout its history, the RSC has augmented its central operations with national and international tours, films, television programmes, commercial transfers and fringe activities. It has won over 200 national and international awards including most recently the Queen's Award for Export – but despite box office figures which, it is thought, have no equal anywhere in the world, the costs of RSC activities cannot be recouped from ticket sales alone. We rely on assistance from the Arts Council of Great Britain, amounting to about 40% of our costs in any one year, from work in other media and, increasingly, from commercial sponsorship. To find out more about the RSC's activities and to make sure of priority booking for our productions, why not become a member of the Company's Mailing List. Details of how to apply can be found in the theatre foyer.

CAST IN ORDER OF APPEARANCE

Manly	**David Calder**	**Musicians**	
My Lord Plausible	**Tom Fahy**	Harpsichord	**John Woolf**
First Sailor	**Trevor Gordon**	Violins	**Richard Springate**
Second Sailor	**Kevin Doyle**		**Gillian Springate**
Freeman	**Oliver Cotton**	'Cello	**Alan Carus-Wilson**
Fidelia	**Geraldine Alexander**		
The Widow Blackacre	**Marjorie Yates**	Music by	**Henry Purcell**
Jerry Blackacre	**Jason Watkins**	Arranged and adapted by	**Guy Woolfenden**
Olivia	**Joanne Pearce**		
Eliza	**Jaye Griffiths**		
Lettice	**Cissy Collins**	Directed by	**Ron Daniels**
Olivia's Boy	**Anthony Dixon**	Designed by	**David Fielding**
Olivia's Maid	**Kathleen Christof**	Movement Director	**Jane Gibson**
Novel	**Mark Hadfield**	Lighting by	**Wayne Dowdeswell**
Major Oldfox	**Nicholas Smith**	Fight Director	**Malcolm Ranson**
Alderman	**Edward Peel**	Music Director	**John Woolf**
Quaint	**Kathleen Christof**	Assistant Director	**Katie Mitchell**
Splitcause	**Cissy Collins**	Stage Manager	**Michael Dembowicz**
Petulant	**Kevin Doyle**	Deputy Stage Manager	**Ian Barber**
Bookseller's Boy	**Anthony Dixon**	Assistant Stage Manager	**Sarah West Stevens**
Vernish	**Edward Peel**		
First Knight of the Post	**Kevin Doyle**		
Second Knight of the Post	**Cissy Collins**		
Waitress	**Kathleen Christof**		
Waiter	**Anthony Dixon**		
Bailiff	**Trevor Gordon**		

First performance of this production: Swan Theatre, Stratford-upon-Avon, 20 April 1988.

Please do not smoke or use cameras or tape recorders in the auditorium. And please remember that noise such as whispering, coughing, rustling programmes and the bleeping of digital watches can be distracting to performers and also spoils the performance for other members of the audience.

Arts Council Funded

Biographies

GERALDINE ALEXANDER *Fidelia*
Born: Leamington Spa. **Trained:** Royal Academy of Dramatic Art.
Theatre: Alizon in *The Lady's Not for Burning*, Miss Pirdie in *Miss in her Teens*, Elsie in *Laburnum Grove* (Pitlochry Festival Theatre), Wendy in *Peter Pan* (Bristol Old Vic), Ophelia in *Hamlet*, Shiela Birling in *An Inspector Calls* (Royal Exchange, Manchester and UK tour). Heavenly Finlay in *Sweet Bird of Youth* (Haymarket, London and tour).
RSC: Fidelia in *The Plain Dealer*, Lady Anne in *Richard III*.
Television: *Killer and Taggart, Dr Who, Minder, You Can't Live On Cake, The Gay Lord Quex, A Very Peculiar Practice, Sleeping Murder, Bust, Hannay: A Point of Honour.*
Film: *The Nightingale Saga, The Wall of Tyranny.*
Radio: *One Thing More or Caedman Construed.*

DAVID CALDER *Manly*
Born: Portsmouth. **Trained:** Bristol Old Vic Theatre School.
Theatre: Was member of National Youth Theatre. Seasons at Bristol, Coventry, Lancaster, York, Traverse Edinburgh and Manchester, including Eddie Carbone in *A View from the Bridge*, Shylock in *The Merchant of Venice*, title roles in *Macbeth* and *Butley*, Leonard Brazil in *City Sugar*, Roma in *The Resistible Rise of Arturo Ui*, *Sleuth*, *Accounts*, premiere of Fassbinder's *Bremen Coffee* (Hampstead), Iago in *Othello* (Young Vic), Gorky in *Futurists* (NT), *Ripen Our Darkness* (Royal Court), *Beggar's Opera* (Piccadilly), *Medea* (Riverside), Perchyk in *Fiddler on the Roof* (Her Majesty's). Tours of *Edward II* and *Richard II* in UK, Austria and Czechoslovakia with Prospect Theatre Company.
RSC: Includes *Othello*, *Henry V* (Japan), Lorenzo in *The Merchant of Venice*, Cassio in *Othello*, Chorus in *Henry V*, Balin in *Island of the Mighty*, Krivoy Zob in *The Lower Depths*. This season Manly in *The Plain Dealer*, York in *Henry VI Parts 1 and 2*.
Television: Includes *Wynne and Penkovsky, Tumbledown, Star Cops*, Trial of Klaus Barbie, *That Uncertain Feeling, Good as Gold, Minder, Widows, Blackstuff, Bergerac, Bread or Blood.*
Film: *Defence of the Realm, Moonlighting, Superman I.*
Radio: Includes *Pearl* by John Arden.

KATHLEEN CHRISTOF *Olivia's Maid/Quaint/Waitress*
Trained: Bristol Old Vic Theatre School.
Theatre: Lady Rumpers in *Habeas Corpus*, Jacquenetta in *Love's Labour's Lost*, Lady Sneerwell in *The School for Scandal* (B.O.V.T.S).
RSC: Olivia's Maid/Quaint/Waitress in *The Plain Dealer*.
Radio: *A Midsummer Night's Dream.*
Other: Directed *Adaptation* at B.O.V.T.S.

CISSY COLLINS *Lettice*
Born: London. **Trained:** Welsh College of Music and Drama.
Theatre: Founder member of Fresh Claims Theatre Company. Jan in *The Promotion of Joe Prudential*, Doreen in *Solitary Confinement* (Made in Wales Company, Cardiff). Pauline Mole in *The Secret Diary of Adrian Mole* (UK tour).
RSC: Emilie in *Les Liaisons Dangereuses* (Ambassadors, London and the Music Box, Broadway). This season: Lettice in *The Plain Dealer*, Simpcox's Wife in *Henry VI Parts 1 and 2* and *Richard III*.
Television: *District Nurse, On the Fringe.*

OLIVER COTTON *Freeman*
Born: London. **Trained:** Drama Centre, London.
Theatre: Seasons at Cheltenham, Watford and Edinburgh. At the Royal Court, London: *The Local Stigmatic, It's My Criminal, The Tutor, The Enoch Show, Erogenous Zones, Sport of My Mad Mother, The Duchess of Malfi, Lear, Bingo, Captain Dates Left Sock.* NT: *Love for Love, The Storm, The Royal Hunt of the Sun, Rosencrantz and Guildenstern Are Dead, Much Ado About Nothing, As You Like It, In His Own Write, Oedipus, Edward II, Volpone, Hamlet, Tamburlaine, No Man's Land, Tales from the Vienna Woods, The Madras House, Julius Caesar, The Passion, The Force of Habit, Half Life, The World Turned Upside Down, Despatches.* Teddy in *The Homecoming* (Garrick), James Leeds in *Children of a Lesser God* (Albery), David in *Benefactors* (Vaudeville). *The Speakers* (Joint Stock UK Tour), *That Summer* (Hampstead Theatre).
RSC: John Abud in *The Marrying of Ann Leete*. This season: Freeman in *The Plain Dealer*, Suffolk in *Henry VI Part 1*, Jack Cade in *Henry VI Part 2*, Buckingham in *Richard III*.
Television: *Henry VIII, The Madness, Lovejoy, The Borgias, The Year of the French, Robin of Sherwood, Room at the Bottom, The Party.*
Film: *The Day that Christ Died, Firefox, Oliver Twist, Eleni, The Sicilian, Hiding Out, Here We Go Round the Mulberry Bush.*

RON DANIELS *Director*
Theatre: Associate Director of the RSC. *The Long and the Short and the Tall, Bang, Female Transport, The Motor Show, The National Cause, Ashes, The Samaritan, The Beastly Beatitudes of Balthasar B., Across from the Garden of Allah*, (London), *Afore Night Come, Bingo, Ivanov, Puntila and his Servant Matti, Man is Man, Romeo and Juliet, Camille* (USA).
RSC: *Afore Night Come, Destiny, 'Tis Pity She's A Whore, The Lorenzaccio Story, the Sons of Light, Women-Pirates, Hippolytus, Pericles, The Suicide, Romeo and Juliet, Timon of Athens, Hansel and Gretel, A Midsummer Night's Dream, Peer Gynt, Julius Caesar, The Tempest, Maydays, Camille, Breaking the Silence, Hamlet, Real Dreams, The Danton Affair, Much Ado About Nothing* (1986 Regional Tour), *They Shoot Horses Don't They?*. This season: *The Plain Dealer*.

ANTHONY DIXON *Olivia's Boy/Bookseller's Boy/Waiter*
Born: Black Country. **Trained:** Guildhall School of Music and Drama.
Theatre: Seasons with Wolsey Theatre, Ipswich. Zak in *Dirty Rascals*. Wayne Erickson in *What Name the Peacock Shirt* (Lyric Studio), Calvin in *Cricket at Camp David* (Derby Studio). UK tour as Lennox in *Macbeth*, with Cheek by Jowl.
RSC: This season Olivia's Boy/Bookseller's Boy/Waiter in *The Plain Dealer*.

WAYNE DOWDESWELL *Lighting*
Theatre: *The Fantasticks, Salad Days*, Verdi's *Macbeth, Nabucco* and *Aida*. Mozart's *Cosi Fan Tutte, Don Giovanni* (Sheffield University Theatre), *No More Sitting on the Old School Bench, Painted Veg and Parkinson, Fanshen, The Hunchback of Notre Dame, A Man for All Seasons* (Manchester Contact Theatre), Co-Producers Tours 1987/88: *Not About Heroes, Knuckle, Macbeth*.
RSC: Joined The RSC in 1978. Worked at TOP as Deputy Chief Electrician and Chief Electrician. TOP productions include *Money, Golden Girls, Desert Air, Today, The Dillen, Mary After the Queen, The Quest*. Pit productions: *Deathwatch/The Maids, Speculators*. Currently Resident Lighting Designer at the Swan Theatre – *The Two Noble Kinsmen. Every Man In His Humour, The Rover, The Fair Maid of the West, Hyde Park, Titus Andronicus, The Jew of Malta*. This season: *The Constant Couple, The Plain Dealer*.

KEVIN DOYLE *Petulant/Second Sailor/First Knight of the Post*
Born: Birmingham. **Trained:** Guildhall School of Music and Drama.
Theatre: *Cymbeline*, Startop in *Great Expectations*, Treherne in *The Admirable Crichton* (Royal Exchange, Manchester). Piers in *Hole in the Top of the World*, (Orange Tree, Richmond). UK Tours of *The Miser* (as Cleante), Simon Bliss in *Hay Fever* with Cambridge Theatre Company, and *A Man For All Seasons* with Great Eastern Stage.
RSC: Petulant/Second Sailor/First Knight of the Post in *The Plain Dealer*.
Television: *Keep on Running, Blott on the Landscape, Auf Wiedersehen, Pet, Shine on Harvey Moon, Sharing Time, Coronation Street.*

TOM FAHY *My Lord Plausible*
Born: Birmingham. **Trained:** Central School of Speech and Drama.
Theatre: Seasons at Leicester, Dundee, Perth, Bristol, Salisbury, Worcester, Pitlochry, Chichester and Birmingham, including Leporello in *Don Juan*, Duane Wilson in *Harvey*, Count Skriczevinsky in *Flare Path*, Ross/Bishop How in *The Elephant Man*, Coachman in *On the Razzle*, John Dory in *Wild Oats*, Dolabella in *Antony and Cleopatra*, *King Lear* (Old Vic), *Songbook* (Globe). UK tours of *King Lear* and *The Rivals* with Prospect Theatre Company.
RSC: *Once in A Lifetime*, *Piaf* (both West End). This season: My Lord Plausible in *The Plain Dealer*, Somerset in *Henry VI Parts 1 and 2*, *Richard III*.
Television: *Galloping Galaxies*, *French and Saunders*, *Out of Order*.
Film: *Tess*.

DAVID FIELDING *Designer*
Born: Dukinfield, Cheshire. **Trained:** Central School of Art and Design under Ralph Koltai.
Opera: *Medea* in *Carinto*, *Giovanna d'Arco*, *The Turn of the Screw*, *Hans Heiling*, *La Legenda di Sakuntala* (Wexford Festival). *The Turn of the Screw*, *Il Trovatore* (Welsh National Opera), *Il Seraglio*, *Die Fledermaus*, *Rigoletto*, *Wozzeck*, *The Rise and Fall of the City of Mahagonny* (Scottish Opera). *Ruddigore*, *The Marriage of Figaro*, *King Priam* (also filmed). *Rienzi*, *Mazeppa*, *Xerxes*, *Simon Boccanegra* (English National Opera). *Der Fliegende Holländer* (Royal Opera House). *The Rake's Progress* (Netherlands Opera), *Werther* (Nancy Opera), *Iolanthe* (Komische Oper, East Berlin), *Don Carlos* (staged performance by San José Symphony at Longbeach, *Idomeneo* (Vienna State Opera), *Jules César* (Paris Opera). Future work includes *Street Scene* (Scottish Opera/English National Opera), designing and producing *Elisa e Claudio* for Wexford Festival, *Wozzeck* (Los Angeles Opera).
Theatre: 1971 Head of Design for Theatre Royal York where he designed *Entertaining Mr Sloane*, *Hamlet*, *Equus*.
RSC: This season: *The Plain Dealer*. *The Tempest*, *Restoration*.

JANE GIBSON *Movement*
Theatre: Directed *The Country Wife*, *Loot*, *The Fireraisers*, *The Bald Prima Donna*, *The Lover* (LAMDA). Co-directed *Lark Rise* (Leicester Haymarket, Almeida), *Nana* (Shared Experience) with Sue Lefton, Movement and Choreography for *Cinderella* (Citizens Theatre Glasgow), *Love for Love* (Vancouver), *Cinders* (Royal Court), *One Flew Over the Cuckoo's Nest* (Royal Exchange, Manchester), *The Genius* (Royal Court), *Hot Time* (Common Stock), *Music to Murder By*, *Animal* (Nuffield Theatre, Southampton), *The Beaux Stratagem* (Lyric Theatre, Hammersmith), *A Matter of Life and Death* (NT), *Lear* (Victoria College of Art, Melbourne), *The Pied Piper*, *School for Wives*, *Yerma* (NT), *Lear* (Shakespeare and Company USA).
RSC: *The Revenger's Tragedy*. This season *Much Ado About Nothing*, *Macbeth*, *Plain Dealer*.
Television: Movement and Choreography for *The Borgias*, *Dancing Country* with Sue Lefton.

TREVOR GORDON *First Sailor/Bailiff*
Theatre: *It's A Woman's Place*, *The Nail Makers* (Birmingham), *The Mark Twain Show*, *Wheels*, *Injury Time*, *In Need of Care*, *Puzzles*, *Frankie's Friends*, *Billy the Kid*, *Breaking Chains*, *The Zulu Hut Club*, *Hidden Meanings* (London). *Marathon Madness*, *Chairperson*, *Peace Maker* (UK tours), Patrick in *Black Sheep* (Temba Theatre Co at Young Vic Studio).
RSC: Pastoral Servant in *The Winter's Tale*, Stephano in *The Rover*, Stanley in *Flight*, Drawer/Sailor/Spanish Prisoner in *The Fair Maid of the West*, Armand in *The Balcony*, Deacon in *The Great White Hope*. This season: First Sailor/Bailiff in *The Plain Dealer*, Smith the Weaver in *Henry VI Part 2*, Citizen in *Richard III*.
RSC Festivals: Zach in *The Blood Knot*, *Ogun Abibiman*.

Television: *Empire Road*, *Buccaneer*, *Angels*.
Film: *Management of Discipline* (local government training film).

JAYE GRIFFITHS *Eliza*
Trained: Guildhall School of Music and Drama.
Theatre: *Antony and Cleopatra*, *The Scarlet Pimpernel* (Chichester Festival Theatre), Rosa in *A Moon on a Rainbow Shawl* (Stratford East).
RSC: This season: Eliza in *The Plain Dealer*, Lady Bona in *Henry VI Parts 1 and 2* and *Richard III*.
Television: *A Killing on the Exchange*, *Hard Cases*, *Daimen and Debbie*, *Rockliffe's Babies*, *Watch*, *Storytime*, *Who Cares?*

MARK HADFIELD *Novel*
Theatre: Seasons at Stoke, Derby, Coventry, Sheffield, Newbury, Bristol and Fareham including Puck in *A Midsummer Night's Dream*, Fitz in *Savage Amusement*, Blifil in *Tom Jones*, Dvornichek in *Rough Crossing*, Billy Bibbet in *One Flew Over The Cuckoo's Nest*, Lieut. Colbert in *While The Sun Shines* (Churchill and Yvonne Arnaud), Linus/Snoopy in *Snoopy the Musical* (Duchess), Stan Laurel in *Blockheads* (Mermaid), Benny Southstreet in *Guys and Dolls* (Prince of Wales), Mercutio/Friar Lawrence in *Romeo and Juliet* (Lyric, Hammersmith), Felix in *An Italian Straw Hat* (Shaftesbury), UK tour of *Guys and Dolls*.
RSC: Dromio of Syracuse in *the Comedy of Errors*, Osric in *Hamlet* (RSC Regional tour 1987). This season: Novel in *The Plain Dealer*, Young Talbot in *Henry VI Part 1*, Young Clifford in *Henry VI Part 2*, First Murderer in *Richard III*.
Television: *Crown Court*, *Butterflies*, *The Last Song*.

KATIE MITCHELL *Assistant Director*
Theatre: Started work in theatre as a Production Assistant at the King's Head Theatre. Assistant Director for Paines Plough, The Writer's Company. Also Assistant Director for *Joking Apart* (Belgrade Theatre, Coventry). Directed *Gobstopper* and *Hatikua* (King's Head).
RSC: This season: Assistant Director for *Much Ado About Nothing*, *The Plain Dealer*.

JOANNE PEARCE *Olivia*
Born: Cornwall. **Trained:** Guildhall School of Music and Drama.
Theatre: Seasons at Manchester, Bristol, Leicester, including Dorina in *The Beaux Stratagem*, Cordelia in *King Lear*, Miranda in *The Tempest*, Blanche in *Widower's Houses*, Asta in *Little Eyolf*, Alithea in *The Country Wife*, Lady Windermere in *Lady Windermere's Fan*, Isabelle in *Ring Around the Moon*. Tish in *Unsuitable for Adults* (Bush), Desiree in *Pain of Youth* (The Gate), Scilla Todd in *Serious Money* (Wyndhams & New York), Jean in *The Entertainer* (Shaftesbury), Candy Barr in *Love Field* (Bush).
RSC: Olivia in *Twelfth Night*. This season: Olivia in *The Plain Dealer*, Elizabeth, Lady Grey in *Henry VI Part 2*, Queen Elizabeth in *Richard III*.
Television: *Way Upstream*, *Blat*, *The Two Gentlemen of Verona*, *The Comedy of Errors*, *Jumping the Queue*, *Reilly – Ace of Spies*.
Film: *Morons From Outer Space*, *Whoops Apocalypse*.
Radio: *Howard's End*.

EDWARD PEEL *Alderman/Vernish*
Born: Bradford. **Trained:** Rose Bruford College.
Theatre: Seasons at Bolton, Hull, Liverpool, Leeds and Scarborough, including Luther in *Luther*, Jimmy Porter in *Look Back in Anger*, Nipple in *Little Malcolm*, Truscot in *Loot*, Dr Rance in *What The Butler Saw*, Henderon in *After The Rain*, Musgrave in *Sergeant Musgrave's Dance*, Haddock in *No More Sitting On The Old School Bench*. Blacksmith in *The Dragon*, Sea Captain in *Twelfth Night*, Joe Gascoyne in *The Daughter-in-Law* (Royal Court and abroad), Shogo in *Narrow Road To The Deep North* (Royal Court and tour to Poland, Romania, Czechoslavakia and Italy, Morley in *The*

Changing Room (Royal Court and Globe), *Pillion* (Bush Theatre). *State of Affairs* (UK tour).
RSC: Blacksmith in *Children of the Sun*. This season: Alderman/Vernish in *The Plain Dealer*, Hastings in *Henry VI Part 2* and *Richard III*.
Television: *All Creatures Great and Small, Dr Who, Truckers, Coast To Coast, Juliet Bravo, Minder, Sweeney, Out, Comedians, The Jail Diaries of Albie Sachs, By The Sword Divided., The Black Madonna, Days At The Beach, Shogun.*
Film: *The First Kangaroos, Force 10 From Navarone, Lassiter, O'Luck Man, Britannia Hospital.*
Radio: *All Night Out With The Lady, And Jerusalem Was Built Here.*
Other: Theatre In Education, work as theatre director.

MALCOLM RANSON: *Fight Director*
Theatre: Has directed fights in Germany, Norway, Switzerland and Ireland. *The Three Musketeers, The Duchess of Malfi, Hamlet, Entertaining Mr Sloane, As You Like It, Cymbeline* (Royal Exchange, Manchester, *Hamlet* (Royal Court), *Prisoner of Zenda* (Contact Theatre Company), *The Mayor of Zalamea, Spanish Tragedy, Lorenzaccio, Coriolanus, Up For None, The Critic, Hamlet* (NT). *Hamlet* (Royal Exchange), *The Scarlet Pimpernel* (Chichester and West End).
RSC: *Henry IV Parts 1 and 2, The Knight of the Burning Pestle, The Twin Rivals, Macbeth, Henry IV, King Lear,* Bond's *Lear, Peter Pan, Julius Caesar, Twelfth Night, A Midsummer Night's Dream, Romeo and Juliet, Richard III, Red Star, Macbeth, Troilus and Cressida, Les Liaisons Dangereuses* (also West End), *Les Misérables, Romeo and Juliet, Richard II, The Fair Maid of the West, Macbeth, Twelfth Night, The Jew of Malta.* This season: *The Plain Dealer, Macbeth.*
Television: *Henry VI Parts 1, 2 and 3, Richard II, The Critic, Vorpal Blade, Coriolanus, By the Sword Divided, Black Adder, Submariners, Titus Andronicus, Casualty.*
Directing: Co-director, with John Blackmore, and fight director on *Treasure Island* (Newcastle Playhouse), co-director, with Michael Bogdanov, and fight director on *The Sound of Music* (Tokyo).

NICHOLAS SMITH *Major Oldfox*
Trained: Royal Academy of Dramatic Art
Theatre: Sir Tristram in *Dandy Dick,* Wargrave in *Ten Little Indians,* Doolittle in *My Fair Lady,* Jacques in *As You Like It,* Friar Lawrence in *Romeo and Juliet,* Peter Quince in *A Midsummer Night's Dream, The Beggar's Opera* (Windsor). *Saint Joan* (Worcester), *Outside Edge,* The Minister in *Shut Your Eyes and Think of England.* The Ballad singer in *Portrait of a Queen* (Vaudeville and Broadway), title role in *The Mikado* (Cambridge and Prince of Wales), *St. Joan of the Stockyards* (Queens), German Dentist in *Crete and Sgt. Pepper* (Royal Court), Squire Trelawney in *Treasure Island* (Ashcroft Theatre), Edwards in *The Streets of London* (Stratford East). UK tours of *Don't Just Lie There; Say Something, Deadlock,* The Inspector in *Whodunnit, Me and My Girl, Doctor in the House, Coming of Age, Hay Fever.* Numerous pantomimes including The Babes in the Wood (London Palladium 1987).
RSC: This season: Major Oldfox in *The Plain Dealer,* Duke of Exeter in *Henry VI Parts 1 and 2* and *Richard III.*
Television: *Are You Being Served?, Z-Cars, The Avengers, The Saint, The First Churchills, The Scriblerus Club, Wings of Song, And There's More, Paul Temple, Village Hall, Softly Softly, Act of Betrayal.*
Film: *Casanova, The Twelve Chairs, A Walk with Love and Death, Those Magnificent Men in their Flying Machines, Partners in Crime, Baxter, Frankenstein and the Monster from Hell, Dr Jekyll and Mr Hyde.*
Radio: *Poetry Corner.*

JASON WATKINS *Jerry Blackacre*
Born: Shropshire. **Trained:** Royal Academy of Dramatic Art.

Theatre: Seasons at Manchester and Leeds including Count Drufthiem in *Camille,* Jack in *Jack and the Beanstalk.* Stanley in *Professionals, Julius Caesar* (Elephant Theatre, London), Bettario in *Who Gets Slapped* (Riverside Studios London tour), Chris in *Blind Faith* (Soho Poly). UK tours as Lucky in *Waiting for Godot,* Wilson in *Ruffian on the Stair,* and Hamlet workshop with Not the National Theatre Company.
RSC: Jerry Blackacre in *The Plain Dealer,* Sweet Rutland in *Henry VI Part 2,* Second Murderer in *Richard III.*
Television: *Eastenders.* **Film:** *Winter.*
Other: Workshop with Bristol Express Theatre Company, and Edinburgh Festival 1985.

JOHN WOOLF *Music Director*
RSC: Music Director for *Cymbeline, Julius Caesar* (1979), *Othello,* (1979), *Romeo and Juliet, King Lear, The Comedy of Errors, Philistines, Troilus and Cressida, The Winter's Tale, A Midsummer Night's Dream, Hyde Park.* Arranged music for *The Twin Rivals* and *Molière.* This season: *The Constant Couple, The Plain Dealer.*

GUY WOOLFENDEN *Composer*
Theatre: Head of Music for the RSC for which he has composed more than 120 scores. Music for productions at the Comédie Française, Burgtheater, Teatro di Stabile and Den Nationale Scene, Bergen.
Films and Television: *Chester Mystery Plays, Macbeth, Antony and Cleopatra, Comedy of Errors, Work is a Four Letter Word, The Various Ends of Mrs F's Friends, Secrets, Playing Shakespeare, What a Way to Run a Revolution, Heart of the Country.*
Ballet: Composed and arranged *Anna Karenina* and *Three Musketeers* for Australian ballet.
Conducting: Three productions for Scottish Opera. First UK performances of Nielsens's *Saul and David,* Tschaikovsky's *Maid of Orleans,* and Liszt's *Don Sanche.* Concerts with major symphony orchestras in UK and abroad.
Composing: Many works for the concert hall, and recently a children's musical written with Adrian Mitchell *The Last Wild Wood in Sector 88.*

MARJORIE YATES *The Widow Blackacre*
Born: Birmingham. **Trained:** Guildhall School of Music and Drama.
Theatre: Seasons at Liverpool, Bristol, Nottingham, Birmingham. *Small Change,* Sandra in *Touched* (Royal Court), Celia in *As You Like It, Inner Voices* (National Theatre), *Thatcher's Women* (Tricycle), *Night Mother* (Hampstead), *Children of Dust* (Soho Poly). *The Killing of Sister George* (Cambridge Theatre Company Tour), Joint Stock tour.
RSC: *Outskirts, Richard III, Good* (Broadway). This season: The Widow Blackacre in *The Plain Dealer,* Duchess of York in *Richard III.*
Television: Includes *Couples, Change in Time, All Day on the Sands, Marks, Morgan's Boy, A Very British Coup.*
Film: *Priest of Love, Alberts Memorial, Wetherby, Legend of the Werewolf.*

Understudies
Kathleen Christof Fidelia/Lettice, Eliza/Olivia's Boy/Lawyer/Bookseller's Boy/First Knight of the Post
Cissy Collins The Widow Blackacre
Jaye Griffiths Olivia
Anthony Dixon Novel/Sailors/Jerry Blackacre/Quaint/Bailiff/Second Knight of the Post
Kevin Doyle My Lord Plausible/Major Oldfox
Trevor Gordon Vernish/Freeman/Petulant/Alderman
Edward Peel Manly

Sponsored by
Royal Insurance

RSC REPERTOIRE 1988

Stratford-upon-Avon Box Office (0789) 295623

ROYAL SHAKESPEARE THEATRE

Much Ado About Nothing
by William Shakespeare

Macbeth
by William Shakespeare

The Tempest
by William Shakespeare

Henry VI/Richard III
by William Shakespeare

SWAN THEATRE

The Constant Couple
by George Farquhar

The Plain Dealer
by William Wycherley

The Man of Mode
by George Etherege

Restoration
by Edward Bond

THE OTHER PLACE

Across Oka
by Robert Holman

King John
by William Shakespeare
Supported by Hancox
garden machinery

The Love of the Nightingale
by Timberlake Wertenbaker

Campesinos
by Nick Darke

London Box Office (01) 638 8891

BARBICAN THEATRE

The Jew of Malta
by Christopher Marlowe

Supported by Herald Press

Twelfth Night
by William Shakespeare

The Merchant of Venice
by William Shakespeare

Julius Caesar
by William Shakespeare

THE PIT

Cymbeline
by William Shakespeare

Fashion
by Doug Lucie

Temptation
by Václav Havel

The Revenger's Tragedy
by Cyril Tourneur

Titus Andronicus
by William Shakespeare

RSC in the West End

PALACE THEATRE
Box Office (01) 437 6834
Les Misérables
The Victor Hugo Musical

AMBASSADORS THEATRE
Box Office (01) 836 6111
Les Liaisons Dangereuses
by Christopher Hampton

SAVOY THEATRE
Box Office (01) 836 8888
Kiss Me Kate
by Cole Porter

Royal Shakespeare Company

Incorporated under Royal Charter as the
Royal Shakespeare Theatre
Patron Her Majesty the Queen
President Sir Kenneth Cork
Chairman of the Council Geoffrey A Cass
Vice Chairman Dennis L Flower
Advisory Direction Peggy Ashcroft, Peter Brook, Trevor Nunn
Artistic Director and Chief Executive Terry Hands
Direction Bill Alexander, John Barton, John Caird, Ron Daniels,
Terry Hands, Barry Kyle, Adrian Noble
Director Emeritus Trevor Nunn
Director 1988 Stratford-upon-Avon Season Adrian Noble
Director 1988 London Season Bill Alexander

Administration

John Bradley *Technical Services Administrator*
David Brierley *General Manager*
Peter Harlock *Publicity Controller*
James Langley *Production Controller*
Tim Leggatt *Planning Controller*
Genista McIntosh *Senior Administrator*
James Sargant *Barbican Administrator*
William Wilkinson *Financial Controller*

Deputies

Stephen Browning *Publicity (London)*
David Fletcher *Finance*
Gillian Ingham *Publicity (Stratford)*
Carol Malcolmson *Planning*

A major new arts sponsorship
Royal Insurance is proud to be providing £1.1 million to the
RSC over the next three years. The RSC is extremely grateful
for this unique and generous support.

Swan Theatre

Judith Cheston, Tamsin Thomas *Press* (0789) 296655
Peter Cholerton *Property Master*
Mark Collins *Master Carpenter*
Sonja Dosanjh *Company Manager*
Wayne Dowdeswell *Chief Electrician*
Brian Glover *RSC Collection*
Judith Greenwood *Deputy Chief Electrician*
Josie Horton *Deputy Wardrobe Mistress*
Geoff Locker *Production Manager*
Chris Neale *House Manager*
Eileen Relph *House Manager*
Richard Rhodes *Deputy Theatre Manager*
Emma Romer *Publicity*
Graham Sawyer *Theatre Manager*
Ursula Selbiger *Box Office Manager*
Michael Tubbs *Music Director*
John Woolf *Music Director*

Production Credits for The Plain Dealer

Scenery, painting, properties, costumes and wigs made in RST
Workshops, Stratford-upon-Avon. Swan Property Manager Mark
Graham. Production photographs by Clive Barda.

Facilities

In addition to bar and coffee facilities on the ground floor, there is
wine on sale on the first floor bridge outside Gallery 1. Toilets,
including facilities for disabled people, are situated on the ground
floor only.

RSC Collection

Over a thousand items on view: costumes, props, pictures and
sound recordings illustrating the changes in staging from medieval
times to the use of the thrust stage in the Swan, and comparisons of
past productions of the current season's plays. Come and see our
exhibition; browse in the sales and refreshments area – and book a
backstage tour. Open from 9.15 am. Sundays from 12.00.

'The Plain Dealer':
a Critical Commentary
by Simon Trussler

The Compiler

Simon Trussler has contributed the commentaries to nine previous volumes in Methuen's Swan Theatre Plays series. He has been an editor of *New Theatre Quarterly* and its predecessor *Theatre Quarterly* since 1971, and presently teaches in the Drama Department of Goldsmiths' College, University of London. *Shakespearean Concepts*, due from Methuen London in 1989, will be the latest of nearly two-dozen books on theatrical subjects he has written or edited, and he was also founding-editor of the Royal Shakespeare Company's *Yearbook* in 1978, compiling the annual editions until 1985.

Synopsis

The 'plain-dealing' Captain Manly has just returned from fighting the Dutch at sea, having sacrificed most of his fortune sinking his vessel to prevent it being captured by the enemy. Although loyal to his old ship's company, among them a 'little volunteer' he believes to have been cowardly in battle, Manly suspects the sincerity even of his own lieutenant, the open-hearted Freeman — who confirms his suspicions by paying court to the wealthy but obsessively litigious Widow Blackacre. Manly puts his faith only in his bosom friend Vernish and his mistress Olivia, in whose care he has left his remaining funds. But Manly's trust in Olivia is swiftly shown to be misplaced, for she not only scorns his attentions and refuses to return his wealth, but is eager to launch into an affair with his 'little volunteer' — who reluctantly obeys his orders to permit Olivia's advances, until supplanted in her bedroom by Manly himself under cover of darkness. Having thus begun his revenge, Manly leaves his surrogate to make a second assignation, but Vernish, to whom Olivia is secretly married, returns in time to discover that his wife's supposed lover is in truth a girl, Fidelia, who had disguised herself in order to follow her beloved Manly to sea. Freeman, meanwhile, has secured the guardianship of Widow Blackacre's son Jerry, and tricked his way into a share of the widow's wealth. All three, together with the other courtly fops Olivia has been stringing along, are summoned to witness Manly's final humiliation of Olivia — during which the duplicitous Vernish is also unmasked. Manly at last accepts the friendship of the vindicated Freeman, and the heart of Fidelia, who turns out to be a wealthy heiress just come into her own.

Stage History

The first recorded performance of *The Plain Dealer* was given at Drury Lane, recently rebuilt to Wren's designs, on 11 December 1676. Charles Hart played Manly and Edward Kynaston was Freeman, while the role of Olivia was taken by Rebecca Marshall, less well-remembered today but a favourite with Restoration audiences. Elizabeth Boutell — the heroine of *The Country Wife*, and also a specialist in breeches parts — was the first Fidelia, the comedian Joe Haines played Plausible, and Katherine Corey, better known for her Doll Common in *The Alchemist*, was Widow Blackacre. The play received two court performances — at Oxford before Charles II on 21 March 1681, and at Whitehall before James II on 14 December 1685, on which occasion it is said to have jogged the new king into securing Wycherley's release from debtors' prison.

Revivals later in the seventeenth century were relatively few, or so the limited evidence suggests, but new editions of the play appeared in 1681, 1686, 1691, 1694, and 1700, quite possibly following stage revivals, and at least testifying to its popularity with readers. Slightly fuller records from the first four years of the eighteenth century reveal nine performances of *The Plain Dealer*, but it apparently remained unacted from 1706 to 1720, apart from a brief flurry of revivals in 1715-16. However, it was back regularly in the repertoire during the 1720s and 1730s, by which time Charles Macklin gained an early success as Jerry Blackacre, and James Quin had taken on the role of Manly. The play had achieved nearly 70 performances in the course of the century when it was revived at Covent Garden on 24 January 1743, but this was to prove the last production in its original form for nearly two centuries. An expurgated and 'improved' version by Isaac Bickerstaff was moderately successful from the 1760s to the 1780s, but a second new version by John Philip Kemble in 1796, in which he himself played Manly, managed only three performances in its first season, and was thereafter forgotten. There is no record of a further professional London production until 15 November 1925, when one of the experimental play-producing societies of the time, the Renaissance Theatre, presented the play at the Scala Theatre under the direction of Esmé Percy.

William Wycherley: a Brief Chronology

1641 Born (baptised 8 April) at Clive, near Shrewsbury, eldest of six children of Daniel Wycherley, steward to the Marquis of Winchester, and Bethia, a gentlewoman attendant upon the Marchioness.

1656 Sent to France, became a member of the salon of the Marquise de Montausier, and converted to catholicism.

1660 Restoration of Charles II. Wycherley returned to England, briefly attended Queen's College, Oxford, and was reconverted to the Church of England. Nov., entered the Inner Temple.

1664 Jan., probably among the ambassadorial party sent to the Spanish court, returning in Feb. 1665.

1665 Possibly participated in the Duke of York's naval victory at Harwich in the Second Dutch War.

1669 His first published work, the long mock-heroic poem *Hero and Leander in Burlesque*.

1671 March, his first play, *Love in a Wood; or, St. James's Park*, successfully performed by the King's company at the Theatre Royal in Bridges Street, Drury Lane (published 1672). Began his affair with the Duchess of Cleveland, and entered the circle of court wits under the patronage of the Duke of Buckingham.

1672 Feb., *The Gentleman Dancing-Master* (published 1673) played by the Duke of York's company, at their new theatre in Dorset Garden, apparently only for its initial run of six performances. 19 June, appointed equerry to Buckingham, and served under him in the Third Dutch War.

1675 Jan., *The Country Wife* a great success at Drury Lane.

1676 11 Dec., *The Plain Dealer* performed by the King's company at Drury Lane (published 1677).

1677 Addressed verses to Buckingham, in disgrace in the Tower.

1678 Illness, during which he was personally visited by the king, who provided funds for his convalescence in Montpellier.

1679 Appointment as tutor to the King's illegitimate son, the Duke of Richmond, cancelled upon his marriage to the widowed Countess of Drogheda.

1681 Death of his wife, and continuing litigation over her estate.

1682 Despite his *Epistles to the King and Duke*, imprisoned in the Fleet for debt.

1685 Death of King Charles II. Partly in consequence of a performance at court of *The Plain Dealer* on 14 Dec., James II arranged Wycherley's release and gave him a pension of £200 a year.

1687 Reconverted to catholicism.

1688 Abdication of King James II — and cancellation of Wycherley's pension, after which he returned to spend much of his time on the family estates.

1697 Inherited life tenancy of Clive upon his father's death, and returned to London.

1704 Publication of his *Miscellany Poems* in folio, and beginning of his friendship with the young Alexander Pope.

1705 Publication of the verse satire *The Idleness of Business*.

1709 Wycherley's 'To My Friend, Mr. Pope, on His Pastorals' appeared in Tonson's *Poetical Miscellanies*.

1715 Marriage, on his deathbed, to a younger woman, apparently to disinherit his nephew. 31 Dec., died, and buried in St. Paul's, Covent Garden. His *Posthumous Works* published in two volumes edited by Lewis Theobald (1728) and by Pope (1729).

From 'Manly Rage' to 'Barren Abundance'

All four of the plays on which Wycherley's reputation rests were written probably within half-a-dozen years in the mid-1670s — despite some anecdotal evidence for earlier composition passed on by an impressionable young Alexander Pope. Whether Wycherley wrote them for money or for fame remains uncertain. Neither do we know if he would have sustained his reputation had he continued to write plays after the illness which struck him down in 1678 — probably encephalitis, the permanent effects of which upon the brain would account for the progressive deterioration of his memory, and the impairment of his creative abilities evident in all his subsequent work.

Wycherley's father was a self-made squire, an erstwhile steward who had done rather well for himself during his master's absence under the Commonwealth — not at all unlike the sly but uncultured upstarts so often ridiculed in Restoration comedy. The son duly displayed a contempt for his origins that was, in every sense, cavalier — and not least did he despise the legalistic temperament which plagued his father, and to which, through some perverse attraction, Wycherley himself fell victim after his disastrous first marriage and even, posthumously, in consequence of his second. But when Wycherley began to write plays, around his thirtieth year, he was, simply, a young man who had been educated somewhat beyond his station. 'Polished' in France before the Restoration, he had been introduced into the kind of society soon to be emulated on Charles's return to London. Any formal education, presumably under private tuition, was far less important to his future than the influence of the couple in whose care he was placed, the Montausiers of Angoulême. The wife, 'the incomparable Julie', conducted her own provincial version of a Parisian salon, while the husband kept an austere but analytical distance which was to make him the model for Alceste in Molière's *Le Misanthrope*, and quite possibly of Manly in *The Plain Dealer*.

Wycherley was, evidently, an impressionable young man — under such influences a ready convert to catholicism, though no less responsive to the arguments of his protestant tutor Thomas Barlow when he returned to the Church of England during his brief sojourn in Oxford in 1660. Probably in Spain in 1664, as part of the English ambassador's entourage, he would have been introduced to the plays of Calderón, a major influence on his first two plays. And when the Second Dutch War was declared in the following year, Wycherley's experiences at sea — for which we have only the direct evidence of one of his poems — presumably contributed to the rough but honourable naval background of *The Plain Dealer*.

Wycherley's first play touched no such raw edges, confining itself with almost formulaic precision to the pursuit of love and money in Restoration London. Yet, already, *Love in a Wood* warns us against testing Wycherley's brand of Restoration comedy by modern theatrical or, indeed, moral expectations, nurtured by a diet of Shakespeare and nineteenth-century naturalism. The pattern of the play is formal, not developmental, and characters do not change but rather display different aspects of themselves in changing circumstances. The outcome, moreover, is neither reconciliatory nor realistic, but more like the come-uppance expected from a Jonsonian joke — except that here the chief jester is thwarted, and the puritanical usurer gets his girl, as, indeed, does the least attractive of the rakes. As was to become characteristic of Wycherley, moral judgements seem invited, but are not comfortingly affirmed by the workings of poetic or natural justice, or by a distinct authorial point of view.

The success of the play won Wycherley his place at court — partly through the mediation of the king's mistress-emeritus, the Duchess of Cleveland, who took a fancy to the young man, as did her own admirer, the Duke of Buckingham, who was so charmed by his rival's wit that, instead of exposing him, he made him one of his equerries. But Wycherley's second play, *The Gentleman Dancing Master*, proved a failure, and still seems insubstantial when set against all the thickets of plot in *Love in a Wood*. The age-old theme of young lovers thwarting the plans of a foolish father bears the weight of the intrigue, which naturally has to supply the place of anything resembling romance — though again the kaleidoscopic shifts of viewpoint keep one's interests alert, particularly in the heroine Hippolite, presented variously but not inconsistently as victim and virago.

Similarly, in *The Country Wife*, nowadays regarded as Wycherley's comic masterpiece, the eponymous heroine Margery Pinchwife is at once simpleton and pert *ingénue*, dupe and dolly-bird, a creature of animal instincts and of humane sincerity. More significantly, the highly ambiguous 'hero', Horner — whose simulated impotence gives him entrance to all my lady's chambers — is not a figure on whom any definitive judgement can be passed, though critics over the years have tried to 'fix' him at every point between 'devil' and 'innocent', nightmarish embodiment of lecherous evil and 'natural man', along a spectrum of attitudes to sensuality from the healthy expression of mutual desires to the unconsidered object of his own and other's lust. No less is Alithea, often regarded as Wycherley's ideal woman, at once virtuous and very silly. These highly complex characters contrast, of course, with others amongst whom such aspects are, as it were, shared out — Pinchwife obsessively jealous, Sparkish ludicrously complaisant.

Then came *The Plain Dealer*, and soon afterwards illness, a disastrous marriage, and imprisonment for debt. He enjoyed a brief retrieval of his fortunes under James — ironically, it is said, occasioned by a court performance of *The Plain Dealer* early in the king's short reign. But then came frequent retirement to the country, until his father had the decency to die, and the 46-year-old Wycherley came into what was left of his own. He held court at Will's Coffee-House, published some undistinguished verse, and befriended the young Pope, who tried to retrieve his forgetful mentor's poems from the rambling and repetition which seem to have been the marks of his old illness rather than of senility. He outlived Farquhar, whose plays spoke with a new voice: and he died, on New Year's Eve 1715, having written nothing for the stage for the best part of forty years.

'The Scene, London'

Wycherley's plays usually maintain a careful, critical distance from the follies of 'the town' which they display: and so, at first, did he. As a young law student, he would have been required to live in the Temple, to the south of Fleet Street, just within the western boundary of the City of London — the 'square mile' whose financiers, merchants, and tradesmen were generally regarded with some disdain by the court wits and their audiences. This contempt was rooted not simply in the class-conscious superiority of the leisured over those who chose or needed to work for a living, but also in the knowledge that 'the cits' had been among the most enthusiastic supporters of the puritan revolution, and remained, in more subdued fashion, largely of nonconformist inclination. That both the king and his courtiers were often dependent upon them for financial assistance made it, presumably, all the more psychologically necessary that they be portrayed as semi-literate upstarts in the theatre.

Wycherley spent most of his later London life in lodgings in Bow Street, at first close by the Cock Tavern, where Manly and Vernish meet towards the end of *The Plain Dealer*, and a stone's throw from Will's Coffee-House, situated on the western side at the corner of Russell Street. Here, one of the first-floor rooms remained a meeting place for the wits throughout Wycherley's lifetime: but within a decade or so after his death, Bow Street was already too far east to be fashionable, as the West End drifted yet further from the city walls. During the Restoration period, however, the spinal cord of 'the town' was still the Strand, its heart the recently-developed Covent Garden — and its head the court of King Charles in Whitehall Palace, between the Thames and the modish sauntering-place of St. James's Park.

Within these limits most of the action of Wycherley's plays takes place. In St. James's Park was the 'wood' of his first play, *Love in a Wood*, which also sets its scenes at the 'French House', the familiar name for Chatelain's restaurant in Covent Garden, whose 'ordinary' (a sort of communal *table d'hôte*) was much frequented by the wits of Charles's reign. Here, Sparkish and Horner plan to dine in *The Country Wife*, which would have been handy for Horner's lodgings in Russell Street, then as now running eastwards from Covent Garden towards Will's and Bow Street — and, of course, in the shadow of the first Drury Lane Theatre. Roughly to the south, across the Strand, lay the New Exchange, an arcade of shops and coffee-houses no less popular in plays than in real life.

Westminster Hall was a considerably less familiar setting for a play — though its ample dimensions embraced not only the law courts but arcades of booksellers and stationers, making it an appropriate location for the third act of *The Plain Dealer*. Otherwise, Wycherley's last play takes place in the uncertainly-situated lodgings of its central characters — but their speeches are saturated with the local colour of contemporary London, with references to Locket's, another tavern popular for its 'ordinaries' at Charing Cross, to the 'galleries' which were the most popular promenades at court, and to low-life resorts such as 'the fields at Bloomsbury' and, lower still, 'beyond the Tower' where 'suburb mistresses' might economically be kept.

Jerry Blackacre talks in the third act of retrieving his pawned plate 'out of most of the ale-houses betwixt Hercules Pillars and the Boatswain in Wapping', and one of Wycherley's learned editors duly conducts an earnest footnoted enquiry as to whether the Hercules Pillars at Hyde Park Corner or in Fleet Street is intended — plumping for the latter, as likeliest to have been frequented by a young law student. Yet even a good half-century afterwards, Fielding in *Tom Jones* could write of the Hercules Pillars tavern at Hyde Park Corner as 'the first he saw on his arrival in town', and it seems likelier that young Jerry, true to his training, should be stretching his point to its full rhetorical potential, by naming the two pubs of his acquaintance set furthest apart at the very western and eastern extremities of London — both still approached across the green fields which lay beyond Pall Mall and Ratcliffe Highway respectively. The Hercules Pillars at Hyde Park would , besides, have made a good watering-hole on the way back from watching an execution just up the footpath at Tyburn.

Wycherley's London was, then, still a relatively small place, and the West End from which most of his audience would have come still smaller. Although footmen and cits, alike beneath contempt, might occupy the upper gallery of its theatres, the audience that mattered was drawn from the fashionable inhabitants of 'the town', who not only knew one another but were also well acquainted, personally as well as professionally, with the actors. Through them, the theatre touched the court and the king himself — one of whose first acts following the Restoration was to grant the letters-patent to Davenant and Killigrew which, throughout Wycherley's career and for long afterwards, continued to regulate the theatre's existence.

The Altered Face of the Stage

When play-acting returned to London with the Restoration, after being banned by the puritans since 1642, it was at first in improvised theatres, converted from 'real' (or 'royal') indoor tennis courts. Killigrew's company, under the king's own patronage, was the first to move to a purpose-built playhouse, the Theatre Royal in Bridges Street, Drury Lane, in 1663, and it was here in 1671 that Wycherley's first play, *Love in a Wood*, was performed. But just over a year later this theatre was destroyed by fire, and the company found a temporary home in the converted Lisle's Tennis Court in Lincoln's Inn Fields, which had been abandoned by Davenant's old company, the Duke of York's, in 1671 on the completion of their own new playhouse. Designed by Sir Christopher Wren, this was situated in Dorset Garden, south of Fleet Street, beside the Thames and not far from the city wall: and here Wycherley's second play, *The Gentleman Dancing Master*, was performed in 1672. But it was in the new Drury Lane, also built to Wren's design, that *The Country Wife* and *The Plain Dealer* were both first played.

Looking back nostalgically to the Restoration years in 1725, John Dennis remarked that 'They alter'd at once the whole face of the stage by introducing scenes and women'. This was not quite true: the court masques of the Jacobean and Caroline period had employed some elaborate scenery, and the open-air theatres of the Elizabethans had long been giving way to indoor 'private' theatres, with greater potential for technical effects. The difference now was that the proscenium arch formed a 'picture-frame' for the painted perspective scenery, changed by the wings-and-shutters system, which provided a formalized background to Restoration comedy and tragedy.

But it was *only* a background: the actors performed on the extensive apron stage in front of the proscenium, in a relationship with their audiences no less intimate and uncluttered than their forebears. Indeed, Restoration theatres, which seated from around five to eight hundred, were actually smaller than the Elizabethan public playhouses, and their audiences, although not drawn quite so exclusively from a courtly elite as has sometimes been suggested, certainly felt themselves to be part of a social as much as of a theatrical occasion.

Quite how that 'crossing of the boundary' between actor and character, so clearly felt in Restoration prologues and epilogues, affected the acting of the play itself is not certain: but the style would certainly have been presentational rather than realistic — at a time, confessedly, when rituals of 'presentation' were of great importance to everyday courtly behaviour as well. So, with

directors unthought of, and playwrights far less involved in the practical business of mounting a play than their Elizabethan counterparts, the influence of the dancing-master was probably strong in matters of movement and stage grouping.

With just two companies of less than thirty players apiece, acting was thus an exclusive though not prestigious profession, its members as well-known personally to many in the audience as their own acquaintances in the pit or boxes. And, although the patents stressed that the introduction of actresses was a matter of morality — to correct the abuse of men appearing 'in the habits of women' — the intimacy between these players and their audiences was not confined to closeness in the auditorium. It was probably inevitable that, in the absence of a traditional route for women into the profession, some actresses in a licentious age should have achieved their positions through sexual patronage — though it is also indisputable that Elizabeth Barry, despite her path being smoothed by the notorious rake Lord Rochester, became a remarkable tragic actress, while Nell Gwyn, although she owed her early chances to being the mistress of Wycherley's first Manly, Charles Hart, became no less striking a comic actress before she caught the eye of the king.

Other actresses, such as the great Thomas Betterton's wife Mary, were nonetheless able to lead lives of untainted virtue at a time when such behaviour in courtly society was almost eccentric — while the fine comic actress Anne Bracegirdle even managed to sustain a reputation for excessive prudishness in private life. This did not, however, prevent her being thought fair game for predatory males: as late as 1692, an assault on her honour was compounded by the murder of the actor William Mountford, who had tried to intervene on her behalf. Those guilty were not severely punished.

When *The Plain Dealer* reached the stage in 1676, the canon of Restoration drama that has survived in the repertoire of the modern theatre included only Wycherley's own plays, and one or two seldom-revived pieces by Dryden, Etherege, Otway, and Aphra Behn. Vanbrugh and Congreve were schoolboys, George Farquhar not even born. Within a couple of years, in 1678, the 'popish plot' was to distract royal attention from theatrical matters, and by 1682 playgoing had so far declined that the King's and Duke's men merged to form a single 'united company', which was found sufficient for London's theatrical needs for the following thirteen years. Arguably, if there ever was a distinctive mode of 'Restoration comedy' it was, even from the first, slightly 'out of sync' with the mood of the society it reflected, and of the court and the courtiers from whom its patronage and its audiences largely derived.

The King, the Court, and the Courtly Wits

Fashionable London in the early Restoration period was a place of determined, almost desperate gaiety. The holding of strong political and religious convictions had, it seemed, led only to the misery of civil war, and to the austerities of the Commonwealth: to be too serious was tantamount to treachery, and to seek pleasure was thus a mark of the patriot. The hypocrisies of which puritans had stood accused — exemplified in the canting preachers portrayed by Ben Jonson — were repudiated: but so also were most other forms of social restraint. Yet permissiveness bred its own forms of double-talk, and the fine facile courtesies of good breeding in turn attracted the contempt of plain-dealers such as Wycherley created in Manly — himself reputedly relishing the appelation bestowed on him by admirers of his own play.

By the time Wycherley began writing, even self-indulgence had become not so much, perhaps, a duty, but to a degree formulaic. When Charles Lamb described Restoration comedy as 'artificial', he meant to apologise for its excesses by suggesting that they did not reflect a real world: on the contrary, it would seem rather that the 'real world' itself operated by an 'artificial' code. It was seemly and witty to write plays, as even the Duke of Buckingham condescended to do, but not with any appearance of industry. It thus became a matter of some labour to appear casual, in art as in personal behaviour. There was a 'theatricality' in the everyday life of the court that was in part mirrored by and in part fashioned by the plays its frequenters saw and wrote. Most people in fashionable society behaved in public as if they were acting: and actors, generally, were 'playing' characters from fashionable society. Dramatic art did not hold a mirror up to nature, but to people who were busy observing themselves in a mirror of their own devising.

The character of the king would itself have fitted well enough into a Wycherley play. Dour, cynical, and introverted at heart, Charles was yet capable of a wit that could be equally pretty or obscene, callous and kindly by turns: he was every bit as 'morally inconsistent' a character as critics have claimed to find Manly. In exile, he had become accustomed to the semblance of power and responsibility, but without the reality of either — a kind of role-play, we might call it, which was how Charles continued to enact life when the immediacy of kingship was in his grasp. As he strolled, supposedly incognito but recognized by all, into the House of Lords to listen to a debate, he would declare the entertainment as good as a play, and sardonically join in the laughter at veiled references to himself.

A regular visitor at the theatre, Charles himself is said to have lent a hand in the writing of plays, and he also interested himself in matters of casting. He at once encouraged and emulated the open obscenities of Restoration behaviour and language, apparently displaying both as freely among women of good breeding as among his cronies or his concubines. While he did not need to adopt the brilliant sexual subterfuge of Wycherley's Horner — indeed, he littered the nobility with bastard sons — in his treatment of his queen as sexually but not socially subordinate to his long line of mistresses he epitomised the workings of the 'double standard'.

As for the leading courtiers — such men as the notorious Earl of Rochester, Wycherley's mentor Buckingham, and his fellow-playwrights Sedley and Etherege — they were a highly-literate but promiscuous and hard-drinking set. The spirit of the times was such that Rochester could order Dryden to be beaten up in a back alley for an imagined satirical slight; the king himself could instigate an assault upon a parliamentarian who had criticized his mistress; and Rochester and Sedley could attempt to rape an heiress in broad daylight. These were men to whom such violence came as casually as a well-turned epigram. In their everyday behaviour, they walked that uneasy tightrope between rape and seduction, between brutality and the defence of honour, which is an aspect of Manly's character in *The Plain Dealer* as it is of other plays of the period.

Dryden actually attributed the supposed superiority of Restoration drama over Elizabethan to the wit and gentility of the conversations between courtiers and playwrights which provided its model. This hyperbolic claim is no doubt partly attributable to Dryden's own equivocal position at court, since neither he nor Shadwell ever achieved quite the treatment as equals that Sedley and Etherege claimed by rank — and Wycherley alone, it seems, enjoyed by virtue of personality and presence rather than pedigree. Later, of course, Wycherley paid in full the penalty of such precarious acceptance. But at the height of his playwriting fame it was a singular advantage — not least when a puzzled and uncertain audience at the first performance of *The Plain Dealer* took their cue from the 'loud approbation' of Buckingham, Rochester, Dorset and their friends to decide in the play's favour. If the court wits approved, that was enough to launch what John Dennis called the 'sudden and lasting reputation' Wycherley's last play achieved.

Writers and Critics on Wycherley

Comedy is both excellently instructive, and extremely pleasant: satire lashes vice into reformation, and humour represents folly so as to render it ridiculous. Many of our present writers are eminent in both these kinds; and particularly the author of the *Plain Dealer*, whom I am proud to call my friend, has obliged all honest and virtuous men by one of the most bold, most general, and most useful satires which has ever been presented on the English theatre.

John Dryden (1677)

Mr. Wycherley, a famous author of comedies, of which the most celebrated were the *Plain Dealer* and *Country Wife*. He was a writer of infinite spirit, satire, and wit. The only objection made to him was that he had too much. However, he was followed in the same way by Mr. Congreve; though with a little more correctness.

Alexander Pope (c. 1709)

There was Villiers Duke of Buckingham, Wilmot Earl of Rochester, the late Earl of Dorset, the Earl of Mulgrave . . . , Mr. Savil, Mr. Buckley, Sir John Denham, Mr. Waller. . . . When these or the majority of them declared themselves upon any new dramatic performance, the Town fell immediately in with them. . . . And when upon the first representations of *The Plain Dealer*, the Town, as the author has often told me, appeared doubtful what judgement to form of it; the forementioned gentlemen by their loud approbation of it, gave it both a sudden and a lasting reputation.

John Dennis (c. 1725)

Wycherley borrowed Alceste, and turned him — we quote the words of so lenient a critic as Mr. Leigh Hunt — into 'a ferocious sensualist, who believed himself as great a rascal as he thought everybody else'. . . . But the most nauseous libertinism and the most dastardly fraud are substituted for the purity and integrity of the original. And, to make the whole complete, Wycherley does not seem to have been aware that he was not drawing the portrait of an eminently honest man. So depraved was his moral taste, that, while he firmly believed that he was producing a picture of virtue too exalted for the commerce of this world, he was really delineating the greatest rascal that is to be found even in his own writings.

W. C. Ward (1888)

Wycherley does not preach, he indicts. To what purpose? To redeem mankind? Hardly, for he has here no example of the happy mean, and indicates no line of conduct to increase social convenience. He is not the preserver of social illusions, nor the wielder of the sword of common sense; nor does he create a fairy world in which all that is necessary is to be comely and to talk wittily. He is far from Etherege, he has thrown off Molière. His laughter affords no release, for it is too deeply cynical; it is of the kind that is man's defence against complete disillusion, but it is too twisted to purge of discontent.

Bonamy Dobrée (1924)

The comments of Wycherley's contemporaries about plain dealing in general and this character in particular suggest that they regarded Manly as a predominantly admirable figure — brave, honest, and intelligent; imprudent, but not ridiculous nor unduly disagreeable. . . . It is probable that what now appears as repellent harshness in Manly was not so unpleasant to his contemporaries. The similarity in tone between the court wits' own satires and Manly's diatribes suggests that they would have interpreted them as Manly himself does — as plain dealing.

Katharine M. Rogers (1972)

Critics rate him highly for different and contradictory reasons. V. O. Birdsall thinks he is a free spirit; Rose Zimbardo sees only a serious, moral satirist; Norman Holland believes that Wycherley is artfully didactic; Bonamy Dobrée, who founded the vogue for Wycherley, sees in him a near-tragic intensity; and Gerald Weales identifies him as a burlesque *farceur*. The conclusion one would have to reach from these contrary views is that Wycherley is a complex enough writer to allow not only such disagreements but also a radical variety of basic misunderstandings. Every man to his own Rorschach, says Gerald Weales. Can a historical interpretation help us see Wycherley as some of his contemporaries saw him? An understanding of his context undermines many of the modern views. One cannot ignore the heavily formulaic element in these plays, especially in the first two, but even working within the conventions of Restoration drama, Wycherley is increasingly able to communicate a dark but ultimately comic view of human experience.

Arthur H. Scouten (1976)

Deconstructing 'Restoration Comedy'?

Critics often use the term 'Elizabethan drama' intending for convenience to embrace the Jacobean besides: but nobody would therefore assume Webster to be coming from the same background as Marlowe, or talk of Massinger in quite the same breath as Thomas Kyd. Yet when Bonamy Dobrée published his long-influential study of *Restoration Comedy* in 1924, and almost unthinkingly took the period from 1660 to 1720 as his catchment area, he was perpetuating a false 'periodization' which went back to Hazlitt and Lamb. The critical tendency persists to treat Vanbrugh and Congreve, if not Farquhar as well, as 'Restoration' dramatists, though none began to write plays until well into the 1690s.

A less obviously fallacious pursuit has been to explore the development not of 'Restoration comedy' but of something called the 'comedy of manners', in which Congreve's work in general and *The Way of the World* in particular is perceived as representing the peak of some Darwinian process of comic evolution. Depending on one's choice of model, *The Plain Dealer* can thus be variously regarded as a late comedy of humours on the Jonsonian pattern, as an early comedy of manners subject to improvement by Congreve, or as falling on either side of the line drawn by Dryden between comedy as corrective satire and comedy as a display of wit.

Of course, the argument becomes even more contentious when moral criteria get mixed into the generic punchbowl. Even Congreve, in this view, falls victim to a vague, Leavisite criterion of 'maturity' — for which, tongue nowhere near his cheek, L. C. Knights proposed as his exemplar Henry James. In his famous attack on Restoration comedy, Knights even quoted with apparent approval a remark by Jeremy Collier, who, in his notorious attack on the morality of the English stage published in 1698, deplored the titillating effects of the sexual chases in Restoration comedy. ''Tis not the success', Collier observed, 'but the manner of gaining it which is all in all'. This, Knights sternly adds, 'of course explains why some people can combine a delighted approval of Restoration comedy with an unbalanced repugnance for such modern literature as deals sincerely and realistically with sexual relationships.' It's bad enough to blame Wycherley for not being Congreve: it is almost surreally unilluminating to expect him to have been D. H. Lawrence.

As it happens, by his contemporaries Wycherley was regarded as a highly moral writer. Dryden, who described *The Plain Dealer* as 'one of the most bold, most general, and most useful satires, which has ever been presented on the English theatre',

elsewhere likened his friend to Juvenal, and even Jeremy Collier, while pausing to censure Manly's irreverent attitude to the nobility, had to 'own the poet to be an author of good sense'. Wycherley was also commended for his characterization — not of contemporary manners, but of humours. And here is a distinction between 'kinds' of comedy which *is* important, because it derives from a perception of the nature and function of the form which is contemporary to Wycherley rather than a product of later thought. 'Humours' were still understood, in the Jonsonian sense, to be affectations or eccentricities, whereas 'wit' required no such individuality for its expression — indeed, depended on an acceptance by sometimes indistinguishable character-types of shared social norms. But few of Wycherley's chief characters can be regarded as fully at home in their society, and when they are 'witty' in the elegant sense of Congreve's characters there is often a creative tension between their individuality and their rhetoric. 'Unbalanced' characters are not best fitted to attempt the 'balance' needed by polished epigrams.

One of the basic beliefs of the so-called 'structuralist' critics of our own time is that there is no direct relationship between language and the 'actuality' it expresses. In this respect Wycherley, whose characters are often the very embodiments of that dissociation, is curiously more 'modern' than Congreve, whose characters *are* precisely what they say. And Wycherley recognizes no less than a modern 'deconstructionist' the fallacy of pinning one's faith to a 'logocentric' perception of the world: into the midst of a society even more verbally-oriented than our own, he thus plunges a Horner to subvert the supposed relationship between language and sexual experience in *The Country Wife*, and a Manly to subvert the supposed relationship between language and social behaviour in *The Plain Dealer*. From that subversion derives both his technique and, of course, the elusiveness of his 'moral purpose'.

A Theatrical Hall of Mirrors

So far from being a 'typical' comedy of manners, *The Plain Dealer* inverts many of the expectations of the form. A couple seemingly clear-cut to fall in love, such as Freeman and Olivia's confidante Eliza, so far from getting married, never even speak to each other. Indeed, marriage in this play seems more like a punishment than a reward — thankfully avoided by Freeman and the Widow Blackacre, but yoking in perpetuity the unhappy Olivia and Vernish. Manly's misanthropy, moreover, rather than being directed against a reasonable man, such as Philinte,

Alceste's butt in *The Misanthrope*, is directed for most of the time against characters who appear entirely to merit his scorn. And when Manly's humour turns misogynistic, it has a nasty, sadistic edge to it, which is not much blunted by the climactic match with Fidelia — who has, after all, for most of the action 'been' a man. The many echoes in the play not only of *Le Misanthrope* — the most often-analyzed source — but of Shakespeare's *Twelfth Night*, in part function to remind us metatheatrically of the artificial quality of *The Plain Dealer*, during which the playwright even offers his audience a lengthy debate between his characters on the morality or otherwise of his own previous play, *The Country Wife*.

And then there's the Widow Blackacre, who ought by all the precedents to be plastering herself with makeup and lusting after every half-way presentable male, but who instead occupies around a quarter of the play indulging her obsession with the law in language which at its vituperative heights achieves a clear Jonsonian ring. She even comes close to defeating Freeman in his designs on her fortune — and as for Freeman himself, surely in setting his sights so low and even then almost missing his target, he is made to look, in James L. Smith's phrase, 'a little cheap'. But does Manly emerge from the action any more creditably? Smith reminds us that one prototype for Manly is the Theophrastan character of 'A Blunt Man' in John Earle's *Microcosmographie* of 1628 — a point valuable not so much for its historical as its typological insight, for it links Manly with a long line of 'malcontents' from the Elizabethan and Jacobean period, whose capricious dispositions seem somehow to surprise critics less than does Manly's.

Thus, Marston's Malevole, in a comedy, gets his wife and his dukedom restored to him, whereas Hamlet, in a tragedy, loses his mistress and his life as well as his father's crown. For the malcontent pursued his misanthropy across generic boundaries, but could only be treated according to the custom of the formal country in which he found himself. So Manly properly gets the girl in breeches who has wandered in from Shakespeare's comedy — and it is quite simply beside the point whether, by his beliefs or his behaviour, he has *deserved* such good fortune, as some critics so earnestly doubt.

In Shakespeare's *Twelfth Night*, there is not one malcontent but two, and both are self-obsessed. One, like Wycherley's father, is a steward with an eye to the main chance, whose name, Malvolio, denotes his typological descent. The other is the Duke Orsino, who thinks he loves Olivia, but who falls readily for the adoring page who has been serving him in male disguise, and who is herself almost exposed when she has no stomach for a fight. There is even a sea captain, who entrusts his purse to the 'male half' of Viola called Sebastian. In *The Plain Dealer*, it is Olivia who suffers humiliation at the end of the play — but she makes her exit at roughly the same penultimate stage of the action as Shakespeare's Malvolio, and both depart vowing their revenge. Where Shakespeare splits his personalities, however, Wycherley reunites them. The steward and the sea captain and the self-indulgent duke are Manly. And Fidelia . . . well, Fidelia is womanly: there is no twin-brother here to marry Olivia, because Olivia is already married to Vernish who has already made off with the purse of *his* bosom-friend.

What a dense, allusive, and elusive play *The Plain Dealer* is! For long stretches, nothing much seems to happen, except for characters displaying their humours in set-piece, Jonsonian fashion. Then, suddenly, the cogs mesh and the wheels whir, and people are dashing about Westminster Hall, groping each other in the fully-lit 'darkness' of the Restoration stage, and chasing all round Covent Garden. Learned modern critics — with the honourable but rather lonely exception of T. W. Craik — tend, however, to forget the action, and to concentrate on the play's 'meaning'. Several have sought to define this in terms of the opposition suggested by the Horatian motto on Wycherley's title-page — 'ridicule often decides great matters more effectively than severity': and a majority have decided that Manly, so far from being Wycherley's satiric spokesman, as most of his contemporaries believed, is in fact the target of this 'ridicule'. Others see Manly rather as the embodiment of his creator's own inability to reconcile his contempt for courtly excesses with his personal indulgence in them, and Katharine Rogers has even found Wycherley guilty of 'fatal inconsistency' in making Manly, as she puts it, 'both butt and hero' of the play.

But Wycherley, so far from being unaware of any such 'inconsistency', is exploiting the tensions it sets up for his own theatrical and metatheatrical ends. No wonder his first-night audience did not know how to respond: and Wycherley heightened the puzzled self-awareness he had aroused by making his play, as Virginia Birdsall put it, 'about both comedy and satire, as well as about realism and idealism.' As Ian Donaldson argues of Manly, but could well be said of the very structure and self-referential quality of the play, its 'contradictoriness' is the source of its 'energy and brilliance'. *Twelfth Night* solutions are all very well, but the characters of *this* play have all just been to see *The Country Wife*. The hall of mirrors lengthens, and nobody is quite sure whether the figures they see — sometimes cowering and squat, sometimes full of spidery motion — are reflections in the distorting glass of the showman or of their own perceptions.

For Further Reading

While the only complete edition of Wycherley's works remains the unsatisfactory *Complete Works* in four volumes edited by Montague Summers (London: Nonesuch Press, 1924; reprinted, New York: Russell, 1966), few readers will require more than the four plays, which are available both in an old-spelling edition by Arthur Friedman (Oxford: Clarendon Press, 1979) and in the more helpfully annotated, modernized *Plays* edited by Peter Holland (Cambridge University Press, 1983). Of earlier editions, that by Gerald Weales (New York: Doubleday, 1966) is superior to (though less widely available than) the old Mermaid edition by W. C. Ward (London: Vizetelly, 1888). There are separate critical editions of *The Plain Dealer* edited by Leo Hughes for the Regents Restoration Drama Series (London: Arnold, 1968), and by James L. Smith for the New Mermaids Series (London: Benn, 1979).

Of the few biographical studies, B. Eugene McCarthy's *William Wycherley* (Athens: Ohio University Press, 1979) is superior to Willard Connely's *Brawny Wycherley* (New York: Scribners, 1930), while Katharine M. Rogers's study in the Twayne's English Authors Series (New York: Twayne, 1972) blends biography with a chronological survey of the works. Full-length critical studies exclusively devoted to Wycherley include the concise monograph by P.F. Vernon for the Writers and Their Work Series (London: Longmans, for the British Council, 1965); W. R. Chadwick's *The Four Plays of William Wycherley* (The Hague: Mouton, 1975); and two works whose approaches are both defined and, it has to be said, limited by their sub-titles — Rose A. Zimbardo's *Wycherley's Drama: a Link in the Development of English Satire* (New Haven, Conn.: Yale University Press, 1965), and James Thompson's *Language in Wycherley's Plays: Seventeenth-Century Language Theory and Drama* (University of Alabama Press, 1984).

Among articles dealing with Wycherley's work in general, the most helpful are T. W. Craik's 'Some Aspects of Satire in Wycherley's Plays', in *English Studies*, XLI (1960); Ann Righter's 'William Wycherley', in *Restoration Theatre*, ed. John Russell Brown and Bernard Harris (London: Arnold, 1965); and Robert D. Hume's 'William Wycherley: Text, Life, Interpretation', in *Modern Philology*, LXXVIII (1981). Articles dealing specifically with *The Plain Dealer* include, in alphabetical rather than evaluative order, Percy G. Adams's 'What Happened in Olivia's Bedroom? or Ambiguity in *The Plain Dealer*', in *Essays in Honor of Esmond Marilla*, ed. Thomas Austin Kirby and William John Oliver (Baton Rouge: Louisiana State University Press, 1971); A. H. Chorney's 'Wycherley's Manly Reinterpreted', in *Essays Critical and Historical Dedicated to Lily B. Campbell* (Berkeley: University of California Press, 1950); Ian Donaldson's 'Tables Turned: *The Plain Dealer*', in *Essays in Criticism*, XVII (1967), reprinted in his *The World Upside-Down* (Oxford: Clarendon Press, 1970); A. M. Friedson's 'Wycherley and Molière: Satirical Points of View in *The Plain Dealer*', in *Modern Philology*, LXIV (1967); Harley Granville-Barker's 'Wycherley and Dryden', in his *On Dramatic Method* (New York: Hill and Wang, 1956); B. Eugene McCarthy's 'Wycherley's *Plain Dealer* and the Limits of Wit', in *English Miscellany*, XXII (1971); and Katharine M. Rogers's 'Fatal Inconsistency: Wycherley and *The Plain Dealer*', in *English Literary History*, XXVII (1961).

General studies of Restoration drama which deal extensively or helpfully (and sometimes even both) with Wycherley include such pioneering early studies as John Palmer's now somewhat outdated *The Comedy of Manners* (London: Bell, 1913), Bonamy Dobrée's stylish but superficial *Restoration Comedy* (Oxford: Clarendon Press, 1924), and Kathleen Lynch's still relevant *The Social Mode of Restoration Comedy* (London: Macmillan, 1926); works of a mid-century flavour such as Thomas H. Fujimura's *The Restoration Comedy of Wit* (Princeton University Press, 1952) and Norman Holland's *The First Modern Comedies* (Harvard University Press, 1959); and more recent studies of which the most notable are Virginia Ogden Birdsall's *Wild Civility: the English Comic Spirit on the Restoration Stage* (Indiana University Press, 1970), Kenneth Muir's *The Comedy of Manners* (London, 1970), Peter Holland's *The Ornament of Action* (Cambridge University Press, 1979), and John T. Harwood's *Critics, Values, and Restoration Comedy* (Carbondale: Southern Illinois University Press, 1982).

Emmett L. Avery's '*The Plain-Dealer* in the Eighteenth Century', in *Research Studies of the State College of Washington*, XI (1943), deals specifically with our play's stage history, and the same author later collaborated with Arthur H. Scouten on the valuably conspective introduction to the first volume of the massive 'calendar' *The London Stage*, reprinted separately as *The London Stage 1660-1700* (Carbondale: Southern Illinois University Press, 1968). Two books which balance theatrical history with dramatic criticism in surveying the whole of the Restoration period (and beyond) are the fifth volume of *The Revels History of Drama in English*, ed. John Loftis *et al.* (London: Methuen, 1976) and Robert D. Hume's *The Development of English Drama in the Late Seventeenth Century* (Oxford: Clarendon Press, 1976).

THE PLAIN DEALER

by William Wycherley

To My Lady B—

MADAM, Though I never had the honour to receive a favour from you, nay, or be known to you, I take the confidence of an author to write to you a *billet doux* dedicatory; which is no new thing, for by most dedications it appears that authors, though they praise their patrons from top to toe and seem to turn 'em inside out, know 'em as little as sometimes their patrons their books, though they read 'em out; and if the poetical daubers did not write the name of the man or woman on top of the picture, 'twere impossible to guess whose it were. But you, madam, without the help of a poet, have made yourself known and famous in the world and, because you do not want it, are therefore most worthy of an epistle dedicatory. And this play claims naturally your protection, since it has lost its reputation with the ladies of stricter lives in the playhouse; and (you know) when men's endeavours are discountenanced and refused by the nice coy women of honour, they come to you, to you the great and noble patroness of rejected and bashful men, of which number I profess myself to be one, though a poet, a dedicating poet; to you, I say, madam, who have as discerning a judgement, in what's obscene or not, as any quick-sighted civil person of 'em all, and can make as much of a double-meaning saying as the best of 'em; yet would not, as some do, make nonsense of a poet's jest, rather than not make it bawdy; by which they show they as little value wit in a play as in a lover, provided they can bring t'other thing about. Their sense indeed lies all one way, and therefore are only for that in a poet which is moving, as they say. But what do they mean by that word 'moving'? Well, I must not put 'em to the blush, since I find I can do't. In short, madam, you would not be one of those who ravish a poet's innocent words and make 'em guilty of their own naughtiness (as 'tis termed) in spite of his teeth; nay, nothing is secure from the power of their imaginations, no, not their husbands, whom they cuckold with themselves by thinking of other men and so make the lawful matrimonial embraces adultery; wrong husbands and poets in thought and word, to keep their own reputations. But your ladyship's justice, I know, would think a woman's arraigning and damning a poet for her own obscenity, like her crying out a rape and hanging a man for giving her pleasure, only that she might be thought not to consent to't; and so, to vindicate her honour forfeits her modesty. But you, madam, have too much modesty to pretend to't, though you have as much to say for your modesty as many a nicer she, for you never were seen at this play, no, not the first day; and 'tis no matter what people's lives have been, they are unquestionably modest who frequent not this play. For, as Mr Bayes says of his, that it is the only touchstone of men's wit and understanding, mine is, it seems, the only touchstone of women's virtue and modesty. But hold, that touchstone is equivocal and by the strength of a lady's imagination may become something that is not civil; but your ladyship, I know, scorns to misapply a touchstone. And, madam, though you have not seen this play, I hope (like other nice ladies) you will the rather read it. Yet, lest the chambermaid or page should not be trusted and their indulgence could gain no further admittance for it than to their ladies' lobbies or outward rooms, take it into your care and protection, for, by your recommendation and procurement, it may have the honour to get into their closets; for what they renounce in public often entertains 'em there, with your help especially. In fine, madam, for these and many other reasons, you are the fittest patroness or judge of this play, for you show no partiality to this or that author. For from some many ladies will take a broad jest as cheerfully as from the watermen and sit at some down-right filthy plays (as they call 'em) as well satisfied and as still as a poet could wish 'em elsewhere. Therefore it must be the doubtful obscenity of my plays alone they take exceptions at, because it is too bashful for 'em, and indeed most women hate men for attempting to halves on their chastity, and bawdy I find, like satire, should be home, not to have it taken notice of. But, now I mention satire, some there are who say, 'tis the plain-dealing of the play, not the obscenity, 'tis taking off the ladies' masks, not offering at their petticoats, which offends 'em. And generally they are not the handsomest, or most innocent, who are the most angry at being discovered:

– *Nihil est audacius illis*
Deprehensis; iram, atque animos a crimine sumunt.

Pardon, madam, the quotation, for a dedication can no more be without ends of Latin than flattery; and 'tis no matter for whom it is writ to, for an author can as easily (I hope) suppose people to have more understanding and languages than they have, as well as more virtues. But why the devil should any of the few modest and handsome be alarmed? (For some there are who as well as any deserve those attributes, yet refrain not from seeing this play, nor think it any addition to their virtue to set up for it in a playhouse, lest there it should look too much like acting.) But why, I say, should any at all of the truly virtuous be concerned, if those who are not so are distinguished from 'em? For by that mask of modesty which women wear promiscuously in public, they are all alike, and you can no more know a kept wench from a woman of honour by her looks than by her dress. For those who are of quality without honour (if any such there are), they have their quality to set off their false modesty, as well as their false jewels, and you must no more suspect their countenances for counterfeit than their pendants, though, as the Plain dealer Montaigne says, *Elles envoyent leur conscience au bordel et tiennent leur contenance en règle.* But those who act as they look ought not to be scandalised at the reprehension of others' faults, lest they tax themselves with 'em and by too delicate and quick an apprehension not only make that obscene which I meant innocent but that satire on all which was intended only on those who deserved it. But, madam, I beg your pardon for this digression to civil women and ladies of honour, since you and I shall never be the better for 'em; for a comic poet and a lady of your profession make most of the other sort, and the stage and your houses, like our plantations, are propagated by the least nice women; and, as with the ministers of justice, the vices of the age are our best business. But, now I mention public persons, I can no longer defer doing you the justice of a dedication and telling you your own, who are, of all public-spirited people, the most necessary, most communicative, most generous and hospitable. Your house has been the house of the people, your sleep still disturbed for the public, and when you arose 'twas that others might lie down and you waked that others might rest. The good you have done is unspeakable. How many young unexperienced heirs have you kept from rash, foolish marriages and from being jilted for their lives by the worst sort of jilts, wives? How many bewitched widowers' children have you preserved from the tyranny of stepmothers? How many old dotards from cuckoldage and keeping other men's wenches and children? How many adulteries and unnatural sins have you prevented? In fine, you have been a constant scourge to the old lecher, and often a terror to the young. You have made concupiscence its own punishment and extinguished lust with lust, like blowing up of houses to stop the fire.

Nimirum propter continentiam, incontinentia
Necessaria est, incendium ignibus extinguitur.

There's Latin for you again, madam; I protest to you, as I am an author, I cannot help it. Nay, I can hardly keep myself from quoting Aristotle and Horace and talking to you of the rules of writing (like the French authors) to show you and my readers I understand 'em, in my epistle, lest neither of you should find it out by the play; and, according to the rules of dedication, 'tis no matter whether you understand or no what I quote or say to you of writing, for an author can as easily make anyone a judge or critic in an epistle as an hero in his play. But, madam, that this may prove to the end a true epistle dedicatory, I'd have you know 'tis not without a design upon you, which is in the behalf of the fraternity of Parnassus, that songs and sonnets may go at your houses and in your liberties for guineas and half guineas, and that wit, at least with you, as of old, may be the price of beauty: and so you will prove a true encourager of poetry, for love is a better help to it than wine and poets, like painters, draw better after the life than by fancy. Nay, in justice, madam, I think a poet ought to be as free of your houses as of the playhouses, since he contributes to the support of both and is as necessary to such as you as a ballad-singer to the pick-purse, in convening the cullies at the theatres, to be picked up and carried to supper and bed at your houses. And, madam, the reason of this motion of mine is because poor poets can get no favour in the tiring-rooms, for they are no keepers, you know; and folly and money, the old enemies of wit, are even too hard for it on its own dunghill. And for other ladies, a poet can least go to the price of them. Besides, his wit, which ought to recommend him to 'em, is as much an obstruction to his love as to his wealth or preferment, for most women nowadays apprehend wit in a lover as much as in a husband. They hate a man that knows 'em; they must have a blind, easy fool whom they can lead by the nose and, as the Scythian women of old, must baffle a man and put out his eyes ere they will lie with him, and then too, like thieves, when they have plundered and stripped a man, leave him. But if there should be one of an hundred of those ladies generous enough to give herself to a man that has more wit than money (all things considered) he would think it cheaper coming to you for a mistress though you made him pay his guinea, as a man in a journey (out of good husbandry) had better pay for what he has in an inn than lie on freecost at a gentleman's house.

In fine, madam, like a faithful dedicator I hope I have done myself right in the first place, then you and your profession, which in the wisest and most religious government of the world is honoured with the public allowance and in those that are thought the most uncivilised and barbarous is protected and supported by the ministers of justice. And of you, madam, I ought to say no more here, for your virtues deserve a poem rather than an epistle, or a volume entire to give the world your memoirs of life at large, and which (upon the word of an author that has a mind to make an end of his dedication) I promise to do, when I write the annals of our British love, which shall be dedicated to the ladies concerned, if they will not think them something too obscene too, when your life, compared with many that are thought innocent, I doubt not may vindicate you, and me, to the world for the confidence I have taken in this address to you, which then may be thought neither impertinent, nor immodest. And, whatsoever your amorous misfortunes have been, none can charge you with that heinous and worst of women's crimes, hypocrisy. Nay, in spite of misfortunes or age you are the same woman still, though most of your sex grow Magdalens at fifty and, as a solid French author has it,

Après le plaisir, vient la peine,
Après la peine la vertu.

But sure an old sinner's continency is much like a gamester's forswearing play when he has lost all his money; and modesty is a kind of a youthful dress, which as it makes a young woman more amiable makes an old one more nauseous. A bashful old woman is like an hopeful old man, and the affected chastity of antiquated beauties is rather a reproach than an honour to 'em, for it shows the men's virtue only, not theirs. But you, in fine, madam, are no more an hypocrite than I am when I praise you, therefore, I doubt not, will be thought (even by yours and the play's enemies, the nicest ladies) to be the fittest patroness for,

Madam,
Your ladyship's most obedient,
faithful, humble servant, and
The Plain Dealer

THE PROGRAMME

In addition to cast list, biographies and play notes, the programme you have purchased for this performance contains the full text of the play. *Please* would you bear in mind that following the text during the performance is very distracting to the performers especially when you are seated in rows close to the stage.

Thank you for your help.

Dramatis Personae

MANLY, *of an honest, surly, nice humour, supposed first in the time of the Dutch War to have procured the command of a ship out of honour, not interest, and choosing a sea life only to avoid the world.*

FREEMAN, *Manly's lieutenant, a gentleman well educated, but of a broken fortune, a complier with the age.*

VERNISH, *Manly's bosom and only friend.*

NOVEL, *a pert, railing coxcomb and an admirer of novelties, makes love to Olivia.*

MAJOR OLDFOX, *an old impertinent fop, given to scribbling makes love to the Widow Blackacre.*

MY LORD PLAUSIBLE, *a ceremonious, supple, commending coxcomb, in love with Olivia.*

JERRY BLACKACRE, *a true raw squire, under age and his mother's government, bred to the law.*

OLIVIA, *Manly's mistress.*

FIDELIA, *in love with Manly and followed him to sea in man's clothes.*

ELIZA, *cousin to Olivia.*

LETTICE, *Olivia's woman.*

THE WIDOW BLACKACRE, *a petulant, litigious widow, always in law, and mother to Squire Jerry.*

LAWYERS, KNIGHTS OF THE POST, BAILIFFS, AN ALDERMAN, A BOOK-SELLER'S PRENTICE, A FOOTBOY, SAILORS, WAITERS AND ATTENDANTS.

The Scene
London

The Text

The text of *The Plain Dealer* is reproduced here in full. The cuts made in the RSC version are indicated by square brackets in the text. Alterations are indicated at the foot of the page.

Prologue

THE PLAIN DEALER.
I the Plain Dealer am to act today
And my rough part begins before the play.
First, you who scribble, yet hate all that write,
And keep each other company in spite,
As rivals in your common mistress, fame,
And with faint praises one another damn;
'Tis a good play (we know) you can't forgive,
But grudge yourselves the pleasure you receive:
Our scribbler therefore bluntly bid me say,
He would not have the wits pleased here today.
Next, you, the fine, loud gentlemen o'th'pit,
Who damn all plays; yet if y'ave any wit,
'Tis but what here you sponge and daily get;
Poets, like friends to whom you are in debt,
You hate, and so rooks laugh, to see undone
Those pushing gamesters whom they live upon.
Well, you are sparks and still will be i'th'fashion;
Rail then at plays to hide your obligation.
Now, you shrewd judges who the boxes sway,
Leading the ladies' hearts and sense astray,
And, for their sakes, see all and hear no play,
Correct your cravats, foretops, lock behind,
The dress and breeding of the play ne'er mind;
Plain-dealing is, you'll say, quite out of fashion;
You'll have it here, as in a dedication;
And your fair neighbours, in a limning poet,
No more than in a painter will allow it.
Pictures too like, the ladies will not please;
They must be drawn too here, like goddesses.
You, as at Lely's too, would truncheon wield,
And look like heroes in a painted field;
But the coarse dauber of the coming scenes
To follow life and nature only means,
Displays you as you are, makes his fine woman
A mercenary jilt, and true to no man:
His men of wit and pleasure of the age
Are as dull rogues as ever cumbered stage;
He draws a friend, only to custom just,
And makes him naturally break his trust.
I, only, act a part like none of you –
And yet, you'll say, it is a fool's part too –
An honest man, who, like you, never winks
At faults but, unlike you, speaks what he thinks.
The only fool who ne'er found patron yet,
For truth is now a fault, as well as wit.

And where else, but on stages, do we see
Truth pleasing or rewarded honesty?
Which our bold poet does this day in me.
If not to th'honest, be to th'prosperous kind;
Some friends at court let the Plain Dealer find.

ACT ONE

Scene One

Captain Manly's lodgings. Enter Captain Manly, surlily, and My Lord Plausible following him, and two Sailors behind.

MANLY.
Tell not me, my good Lord Plausible, of your decorums, supercilious forms and slavish ceremonies, your little tricks, which you the spaniels of the world do daily over and over for and to one another, not out of love or duty, but your servile fear.

LORD PLAUSIBLE.
Nay, i'faith, i'faith, you are too passionate, and I must humbly beg your pardon and leave to tell you, they are the arts, and rules, the prudent of the world walk by.

MANLY.
Let 'em. [But I'll have no leading-strings;] I can walk alone. I hate a harness and will not tug on in a faction, kissing my leader behind, that another slave may do the like to me.

LORD PLAUSIBLE.
What, will you be singular then, like nobody? Follow, love, and esteem nobody?

MANLY.
Rather than be general, like you, follow everybody, court and kiss everybody, though perhaps at the same time you hate everybody.

LORD PLAUSIBLE.
Why, seriously, with your pardon, my dear friend –

MANLY.
With your pardon, my no friend, I will not, as you do, [whisper my hatred or my scorn,] call a man fool [or knave] by signs [or mouths] over his shoulder whilst you have him in your arms. For such as you, like common whores and pickpockets, are only dangerous to those you embrace.

LORD PLAUSIBLE.
Such as I! Heavens defend me – upon my honour –

MANLY.
Upon your title, my lord, if you'd have me believe you.

LORD PLAUSIBLE.
Well then, as I am a person of honour. I never attempted to abuse or lessen any person in my life.

MANLY.
What, you were afraid?

LORD PLAUSIBLE.
No; but seriously, I hate to do a rude thing. No, faith, I speak well of all mankind.

MANLY.
I thought so; but know that speaking well of all mankind is the worst kind of detraction, for it takes away the reputation of the few good men in the world by making all alike. Now I speak ill of most men, because they deserve it, I that can do a rude thing rather than an unjust thing.

LORD PLAUSIBLE.
Well, tell not me, my dear friend, what people deserve; I ne'er mind that. I, [like an author in a dedication,] never speak well of a man for his sake but my own. I will not disparage any man to disparage myself, for to speak ill of people behind their backs is not like a person of honour and truly to speak ill of 'em to their faces is not like a complaisant person. But if I did say or do an ill thing to anybody, it should be sure to be behind their backs out of pure good manners.

MANLY.
Very well; but I, that am an unmannerly sea-fellow, if I ever speak well of people (which is very seldom indeed), it should be sure to be behind their backs, and if I would say or do ill to any, it should be to their faces. I would justle a proud, strutting, overlooking coxcomb at the head of his sycophants rather than put out my tongue at him when he were past me, [would frown in the arrogant, big, dull face of an overgrown knave of business rather than vent my spleen against him when his back were turned, would give fawning slaves the lie whilst they embrace or commend me, cowards whilst they brag,] call a rascal by no other title though his father had left him a duke's, laugh at fools aloud before their mistresses, and must desire people to leave me when their visits grow at last as troublesome as they were at first impertinent.

LORD PLAUSIBLE.
I would not have my visits troublesome.

MANLY.
The only way to be sure not to have 'em troublesome is to make 'em when people are not at home, for your visits, like other good turns, are most obliging when made or done to a man in his absence. A pox, why should anyone, because he has nothing to do, go and disturb another man's business?

LORD PLAUSIBLE.

I beg your pardon, my dear friend. What, you have business?

MANLY.

If you have any, I would not detain your lordship.

LORD PLAUSIBLE.

Detain me, dear sir! I can never have enough of your company.

MANLY.

I'm afraid I should be tiresome. I know not what you think.

LORD PLAUSIBLE.

Well, dear sir, I see you would have me gone.

MANLY (*aside*).

But I see you won't.

LORD PLAUSIBLE.

Your most faithful –

MANLY.

God be w'ye, my lord.

LORD PLAUSIBLE.

Your most humble –

MANLY.

Farewell.

LORD PLAUSIBLE.

And eternally –

MANLY.

And eternally ceremony – (*Aside.*) Then the devil take thee eternally.

LORD PLAUSIBLE.

You shall use no ceremony, by my life.

MANLY.

I do not intend it.

LORD PLAUSIBLE.

Why do you stir then?

MANLY.

Only to see you out of doors, that I may shut 'em against more welcomes.

LORD PLAUSIBLE.

Nay, faith, that shan't pass upon your most faithful, humble servant.

MANLY (*aside*).

Nor this any more upon me.

LORD PLAUSIBLE.

Well, you are too strong for me.

MANLY (*aside*).

I'd sooner be visited by the plague, for that only would keep a man from visits and his doors shut.

Exit, thrusting out My Lord Plausible

FIRST SAILOR.

Here's finical fellow, Jack! What a brave fair-weather captain of a ship he would make!

SECOND SAILOR.

He a captain of a ship! It must be when she's in the dock then [for he looks like one of those that get the King's Commissions for Hulls to sell a king's ship, when a brave fellow has fought her almost to a longboat.]

FIRST SAILOR.

On my conscience then, Jack, that's the reason our bully ta sunk our ship: not only that the Dutch might not have her but that the courtiers, who laugh at wooden legs, might no make her prize.

SECOND SAILOR.

A pox of his sinking, Tom; we have made a base, broken short voyage of it.

FIRST SAILOR.

Ay, your brisk dealers in honour always make quick return with their ship to the dock and their men to the hospitals. 'Tis, let me see, just a month since we set out of the river, and the wind was almost as cross to us as the Dutch.

SECOND SAILOR.

Well, I forgive him sinking my own poor truck, if he would but have given me time and leave to have saved black Kate o Wapping's small venture.

FIRST SAILOR.

Faith, I forgive him since, as the purser told me, he sunk th value of five or six thousand pound of his own with which h was to settle himself somewhere in the Indies, for our merry lieutenant was to succeed him in his commission for the ship back, for he was resolved never to return again fo England.

SECOND SAILOR.
So it seemed by his fighting.

FIRST SAILOR.
No, but he was a-weary of this side of the world here, they say.

[SECOND SAILOR.
Ay, or else he would not have bid so fair for a passage into t'other.]

FIRST SAILOR.
[Jack, thou think'st thyself in the forecastle, thou'rt so waggish; but I tell you then,] he had a mind to go live and bask himself on the sunny side of the globe.

SECOND SAILOR.
What, out of any discontent? For [he's always as dogged as an old tarpaulin when hindered of a voyage by a young pantaloon captain.]

FIRST SAILOR.
['Tis true,] I never saw him pleased but in the fight, and then he looked like one of us coming from the pay-table, with a new lining to our hats under our arms.

SECOND SAILOR.
A pox, he's like the Bay of Biscay, rough and angry, let the wind blow where 'twill.

FIRST SAILOR.
Nay, there's no more dealing with him than with the land in a storm, no-near –

SECOND SAILOR.
'Tis a hurry-durry blade. Dost thou remember after we had tugged hard the old leaky longboat to save his life, when I welcomed him ashore, he gave me a box on the ear and called me fawning water-dog?

Enter Manly and Freeman.

FIRST SAILOR.
Hold thy peace, Jack, and stand by; the foul weather's coming.

MANLY.
You rascals, dogs, how could this tame thing get through you?

FIRST SAILOR.
Faith, to tell your honour the truth, we were at hob in the hall and, whilst my brother and I were quarrelling about a cast, he slunk by us.

SECOND SAILOR.
He's a sneaking fellow I warrant for't.

MANLY.
Have more care for the future, you slaves. Go and with drawn cutlasses stand at the stair foot [and keep all that ask for me from coming up. Suppose you were guarding the scuttle to the powder room.] Let none enter here at your and their peril.

[FIRST SAILOR.
No, for the danger would be the same; you would blow them and us up if we should.]

SECOND SAILOR.
Must no one come to you, sir?

MANLY.
No man, sir.

FIRST SAILOR.
No man, sir, but a woman then, an't like your honour –

MANLY.
No woman neither, you impertinent dog. Would you be pimping? [A sea pimp is the strangest monster she has.]

SECOND SAILOR.
Indeed, an't like your honour, 'twill be hard for us to deny a woman anything since we are so newly come on shore.

FIRST SAILOR.
We'll let no old woman come up, though it were our trusting landlady at Wapping.

MANLY.
Would you be witty, you brandy casks you? You become a jest as ill as you do a horse. Be gone, you dogs, I hear a noise on the stairs.

Exeunt Sailors.

FREEMAN.
Faith, I am sorry you would let the fop go. I intended to have had some sport with him.

MANLY.
Sport with him! A pox, then why did you not stay? You should have enjoyed your coxcomb and had him to yourself for me.

FREEMAN.
No, I should not have cared for him without you neither, for the pleasure which fops afford is like that of drinking, only good when 'tis shared, and a fool, like a bottle, which would make you merry in company, will make you dull alone. But

how the devil could you turn a man of his quality downstairs? You use a lord with very little ceremony, it seems.

MANLY.

A lord! What, thou art one of those who esteem men only by the marks and value fortune has set upon 'em and never consider intrinsic worth. But counterfeit honour will not be current with me; I weigh the man, not his title. 'Tis not the king's stamp can make the metal better or heavier: your lord is a leaden shilling which you may bend every way, and debases the stamp he bears, instead of being raised by't. – Here again, you slaves?

FIRST SAILOR.

Only to receive farther instructions, an't like your honour: what if a man should bring you money? Should we turn him back?

MANLY.

All men, I say. Must I be pestered with you too? You dogs, away.

SECOND SAILOR.

Nay, I know one man your honour would not have us hinder coming to you, I'm sure.

MANLY.

Who's that? Speak quickly, slaves.

SECOND SAILOR.

Why, a man that should bring you a challenge, for, though you refuse money, I'm sure you love fighting too well to refuse that.

MANLY.

Rogue, rascal, dog.

Kicks the Sailors out.

FREEMAN.

Nay, let the poor rogues have their forecastle jests; they cannot help 'em in a fight, scarce when a ship's sinking.

MANLY.

Damn their untimely jests. A servant's jest is more sauciness than his counsel.

FREEMAN.

But what, will you see nobody? Not your friends?

MANLY.

Friends – I have but one, and he, I hear, is not in town; nay, can have but one friend, for a true heart admits but of one friendship as of one love. But in having that friend I have a thousand, for he has the courage of men in despair, [yet the diffidency and caution of cowards, the secrecy of the revengeful] and the constancy of martyrs, one fit to advise, to keep a secret, to fight and die for his friend. Such I think him, for I have trusted him with my mistress in my absence, and the trust of beauty is sure the greatest we can show.

FREEMAN.

Well, but all your good thoughts are not for him alone, I hope. Pray, what d'ye think of me for a friend?

MANLY.

Of thee! Why, thou art a latitudinarian in friendship, that is no friend; thou dost side with all mankind but will suffer for none. Thou art indeed like your Lord Plausible, the pink of courtesy, therefore hast no friendship, for ceremony and great professing renders friendship as much suspected as it does religion.

FREEMAN.

And no professing, no ceremony at all in friendship were as unnatural and as undecent as in religion; and there is hardly such a thing as an honest hypocrite, who professes himself to be worse than he is, unless it be yourself, for though I could never get you to say you were my friend, I know you'll prove so.

MANLY.

I must confess I am so much your friend I would not deceive you, therefore must tell you, not only because my heart is taken up but according to your rules of friendship, I cannot be your friend.

FREEMAN.

Why, pray?

MANLY.

Because he that is, you'll say, a true friend to a man is a friend to all his friends. But you must pardon me, I cannot wish well to pimps, flatterers, [detractors] and cowards, stiff nodding knaves and supple, pliant, kissing fools. Now, all these I have seen you use like the dearest friends in the world.

FREEMAN.

Hah, hah, hah – What, you observed me, I warrant, in the galleries at Whitehall doing the business of the place! Pshaw! Court professions, like court promises, go for nothing, man. But, faith, could you think I was a friend to all those hugged, kissed, flattered, bowed to? Hah, ha –

MANLY.

You told 'em so and swore it too; I heard you.

FREEMAN.

Ay, but when their backs were turned did I not tell you they were rogues, villains, rascals whom I despised and hated?

MANLY.

Very fine! But what reason had I to believe you spoke your heart to me since you professed deceiving so many?

FREEMAN.

Why, don't you know, good captain, that telling truth is a quality as prejudicial to a man that would thrive in the world as square play to a cheat, or true love to a whore! Would you have a man speak truth to his ruin? You are severer than the law, which requires no man to swear against himself. You would have me speak truth against myself, I warrant, and tell my promising friend, the courtier, he has a bad memory?

MANLY.

Yes.

FREEMAN.

And so make him remember to forget my business. And I should tell the great lawyer too that he takes oftener fees to hold his tongue than to speak?

MANLY.

No doubt on't.

FREEMAN.

Ay, and have him hang or ruin me, when he should come to be a judge and I before him. And you would have me tell the new officer who bought his employment lately that he is a coward?

MANLY.

Ay.

FREEMAN.

And so get myself cashiered, not him, he having the better friends though I the better sword. And I should tell the scribbler of honour that heraldry were a prettier and fitter study for so fine a gentleman than poetry?

MANLY.

Certainly.

FREEMAN.

And so find myself mauled in his next hired lampoon. [And you would have me tell the holy lady too she lies with her chaplain?]

MANLY.

No doubt on't.]

FREEMAN.

[And so draw the clergy upon my back and want a good table to dine at sometimes.] And by the same reason too, I should tell you that the world thinks you a madman, a brutal, and have you cut my throat, or worse, hate me! What other good success of all my plain-dealing could I have than what I've mentioned?

MANLY.

Why, first your promising courtier would keep his word, out of fear of more reproaches or at least would give you no more vain hopes. Your lawyer would serve you more faithfully, for he, having no honour but his interest, is truest still to him he knows suspects him. The new officer would provoke thee to make him a coward and so be cashiered, that thou or some other honest fellow, who had more courage than money, might get his place. The noble sonneteer would trouble thee no more with his madrigals. [The praying lady would leave off railing at wenching before thee and not turn away her chambermaid for her own known frailty with thee.] And I, instead of hating thee, should love thee for thy plain dealing and, in lieu of being mortified, am proud that the world and I think not well of one another.

FREEMAN.

Well, doctors differ. You are for plain dealing, I find; but against your particular notions I have the practice of the whole world. Observe but any morning what people do when they get together on the Exchange, in Westminster Hall, or the galleries in Whitehall.

MANLY.

I must confess, there they seem to rehearse Bayes's grand dance: here you see a bishop bowing low to a gaudy atheist, a judge to a doorkeeper, a great lord to a fishmonger [or a scrivener with a jack-chain about his neck,] a lawyer to a sergeant-at-arms, [a velvet physician to a threadbare chemist] and a supple gentleman usher to a surly beefeater, and so tread round in a preposterous huddle of ceremony to each other, whilst they can hardly hold their solemn false countenances.

FREEMAN.

Well, they understand the world.

MANLY.

Which I do not, I confess.

FREEMAN.

But, sir, pray believe the friendship I promise you real, whatsoever I have professed to others. Try me at least.

MANLY.

Why, what would you do for me?

FREEMAN.

I would fight for you.

MANLY.

That you would do for your own honour. But what else?

FREEMAN.

I would lend you money, if I had it.

MANLY.

To borrow more of me another time. That were but putting your money to interest; a usurer would be as good a friend. But what other piece of friendship?

FREEMAN.

I would speak well of you to your enemies.

MANLY.

To encourage others to be your friends by a show of gratitude. But what else?

FREEMAN.

Nay, I would not hear you ill spoken of behind your back by my friend.

MANLY.

Nay, then thou'rt a friend indeed. But it were unreasonable to expect it from thee as the world goes now, when new friends, iike new mistresses, are got by disparaging old ones.

Enter Fidelia

But here comes another will say as much at least. Dost not thou love me devilishly too, my little volunteer, as well as he or any man can?

FIDELIA.

Better than any man can love you, my dear captain.

MANLY.

Look you there. I told you so.

FIDELIA.

As well as you do truth or honour, sir, as well.

MANLY.

Nay, good young gentleman, enough, for shame. Thou hast been a page, by thy flattering and lying, to one of those praying ladies who love flattery so well they are jealous of it, and wert turned away for saying the same things to the old housekeeper for sweetmeats as you did to your lady; for thou flatterest everything and everybody alike.

FIDELIA.

You, dear sir, should not suspect the truth of what I say of you, though to you. Fame, the old liar, is believed when she speaks wonders of you. You cannot be flattered, sir; your merit is unspeakable.

MANLY.

Hold, hold, sir, or I shall suspect worse of you, [that you have been a cushion-bearer to some state hypocrite and turned away by the chaplains for out-flattering their probation sermons for a benefice.]

FIDELIA.

Suspect me for anything, sir, but the want of love, faith and duty to you, the bravest, worthiest of mankind. Believe me, I could die for you, sir.

MANLY.

Nay, there you lie, sir. Did I not see thee more afraid in the fight than the chaplain of the ship or the purser that bought his place?

FIDELIA.

Can he be said to be afraid that ventures to sea with you?

MANLY.

Fie, fie, no more. I shall hate thy flattery worse than thy cowardice, nay, than thy bragging.

FIDELIA.

Well, I own then I was afraid, mightily afraid; yet for you I would be afraid again, an hundred times afraid. Dying is ceasing to be afraid, and that I could do sure for you and you'll believe me one day. (*Weeps.*)

FREEMAN.

Poor youth! Believe his eyes if not his tongue; he seems to speak truth with them.

MANLY.

What, does he cry? A pox on't, a maudlin flatterer is as nauseously troublesome as a maudlin drunkard. No more, you little milksop, do not cry. I'll never make thee afraid again, for of all men, [if I had occasion,] thou shouldst not be my second and, when I go to sea again, thou shalt venture thy life no more with me.

FIDELIA.

Why, will you leave me behind then? (*Aside.*) If you would preserve my life, I'm sure you should not.

MANLY.

Leave thee behind! Ay, ay, thou art a hopeful youth for the shore only. Here thou wilt live to be cherished by fortune and the great ones, for thou may'st easily come to out-flatter a dull poet, out-lie a coffeehouse or gazette writer, out-swear a knight of the post, out-watch a pimp, out-fawn a rook, out-promise a lover, out-rail a wit and out-brag a sea-captain. All this thou canst do, because thou'rt a coward, a thing I hate; therefore thou'lt do better with the world than with me and these are the good courses you must take in the world. There's good advice, at least, at parting. Go and be happy with't.

FIDELIA.
Parting, sir! O let me not hear that dismal word.

MANLY.
If my words frighten thee, be gone the sooner, for, to be plain with thee, cowardice and I cannot dwell together.

FIDELIA.
And cruelty and courage never dwelt together, sure, sir. Do not turn me off to shame and misery, for I am helpless and friendless.

MANLY.
Friendless! There are half a score friends for thee then. (Offers her gold.) I leave myself no more. They'll help thee a little. Be gone, go; I must be cruel to thee (if thou call'st it so) out of pity.

FIDELIA.
If you would be cruelly pitiful, sir, let it be with your sword, not gold.

Exit.

[*Enter First Sailor.*

FIRST SAILOR.
We have with much ado turned away two gentlemen who told us forty times over their names were Mr Novel and Major Oldfox.

MANLY.
Well, to your post again.

Exit Sailor

But how come those puppies coupled always together?

FREEMAN.
O, the coxcombs keep each other company to show each other, as Novel calls it, or, as Oldfox says, like two knives to whet one another.

MANLY.
And set other people's teeth on edge.]

Enter Second Sailor.

SECOND SAILOR.
Here is a woman, an't like your honour, scolds and bustles with us to come in, [as much as a seaman's widow at the Navy Office.] Her name is Mrs Blackacre.

MANLY.
That fiend too!

FREEMAN.
The Widow Blackacre, is it not? That litigious she-pettifogger, who is at law and difference with all the world; but I wish I could make her agree with me in the church. They say she has fifteen hundred pounds a year jointure and the care of her son, that is, the destruction of his estate.

MANLY.
Her lawyers, attornies and solicitors have fifteen hundred pound a year whilst she is contented to be poor to make other people so, for she is as vexatious as her father was, the great attorney, [nay, as a dozen Norfolk attornies,] and as implacable an adversary as a wife suing for alimony [or a parson for his tithes, and] she loves an Easter term, or any term, not as other country ladies do, to come up to be fine, cuckold their husbands, and take their pleasure, for she has no pleasure but in vexing others and is usually clothed and daggled like a bawd in disguise, pursued through alleys by sergeants. When she is in town she lodges in one of the Inns of Chancery, where she breeds her son and is herself his tutoress in law-French, [and for her country abode, though she has no estate there, she chooses Norfolk.] But bid her come in, with a pox to her. She is Olivia's kinswoman and may make me amends for her visit by some discourse of that dear woman.

Exit Sailor.

Enter Widow Blackacre with a mantle and a green bag and several papers in the other hand. Jerry Blackacre her son, in a gown, laden with green bags, following her.

WIDOW.
I never had so much to do with a judge's doorkeeper, as with yours, but –

MANLY.
But the incomparable Olivia, how does she since I went?

WIDOW.
Since you went, my suit –

MANLY.
Olivia, I say, is she well?

WIDOW.

My suit, if you had not returned –

MANLY.

Damn your suit. How does your cousin Olivia?

WIDOW.

My suit, I say, had been quite lost, but now –

MANLY.

But now, where is Olivia? In town? For –

WIDOW.

For tomorrow we are to have a hearing.

MANLY.

Would you'd let me have a hearing today.

WIDOW.

But why won't you hear me?

MANLY.

I am no judge and you talk of nothing but suits. But, pray tell me, when did you see Olivia?

WIDOW.

I am no visitor but a woman of business, or if I ever visit 'tis only the Chancery Lane ladies, ladies towards the law and not any of your lazy, good-for-nothing flirts, who cannot read law-French, though a gallant writ it. But, as I was telling you, my suit –

MANLY.

Damn these impertinent, vexatious people of business, of all sexes. [They are still troubling the world with the tedious recitals of their lawsuits, and one can no more stop their mouths than a wit's when he talks of himself, or an intelligencer's when he talks of other people.]

WIDOW.

And a pox of all vexatious, impertinent lovers.[They are still perplexing the world with the tedious narrations of their love-suits and discourses of their mistresses.] You are as troublesome to a poor widow of business as a young coxcombly rithming lover.

MANLY.

And thou art as troublesome to me as [a rook to a losing gamester or] a young putter of cases to his mistress and sempstress, who has love in her head for another.

WIDOW.

Nay, since you talk of putting of cases and will not hear me speak, hear our Jerry a little. Let him put our case to you, for

the trial's tomorrow and, since you are my chief witness, I would have your memory refreshed and your judgement informed, that you may not give your evidence improperly. Speak out, child.

JERRY.

Yes, forsooth. Hemh! Hemh! John-a-Stiles –

MANLY.

You may talk, young lawyer, but I shall no more mind you than a hungry judge does a cause after the clock has struck one.

FREEMAN.

Nay, you'll find him as peevish too.

WIDOW.

No matter. Jerry, go on. Do you observe it then, sir, for I think I have seen you in a gown once. Lord, I could hear our Jerry put cases all day long! Mark him, sir.

JERRY.

John-a-Stiles – no – There are first Fitz, Pere and Ayle – No, no, Ayle, Pere and Fitz. Ayle is seised in fee of Blackacre; John-a-Stiles disseises Ayle; Ayle makes claim and the disseisor dies, then the Ayle – no, the Fitz.

WIDOW.

No, the Pere, sirrah.

JERRY.

O, the Pere. Ay, the Pere, sir, and the Fitz – no, the Ayle; no, the Pere and the Fitz, sir, and –

MANLY.

Damn Pere, Mere and Fitz, sir.

WIDOW.

No, you are out, child. Hear me, captain, then. There are Ayle, Pere and Fitz; Ayle is seised in fee of Blackacre and being so seised, John-a-Stiles disseises the Ayle; Ayle makes claim and the disseisor dies. And then the Pere re-enters, (*To Jerry.*) the Pere sirrah, the Pere – And the Fitz enters upon the Pere, and the Ayle brings his writ of disseisin in the *post*, and the Pere brings his writ of disseisin in the *per* and –

MANLY.

Can'st thou hear this stuff, Freeman? I could as soon suffer a whole noise of flatterers at a great man's levy in a morning but thou hast servile complacency enough [to listen to a quibbling statesman in disgrace, nay, and be beforehand with him in laughing at his dull no-jest.] But I – (*Offering to go out.*)

WIDOW.
Nay, sir, hold. Where's the subpoena, Jerry? I must serve you, sir. You are required by this to give your testimony –

MANLY.
I'll be forsworn to be revenged on thee.

Exit Manly, throwing away the subpoena.

WIDOW.
Get you gone for a lawless companion. Come, Jerry, I had almost forgot we were to meet at the Master's at three. Let us mind our business still, child.

JERRY.
Ay, forsooth, e'en so let's.

FREEMAN.
Nay, madam, now I would beg you to hear me a little, a little of my business.

WIDOW.
I have business of my own calls me away, sir.

FREEMAN.
My business would prove yours too, dear madam.

WIDOW.
Yours would be some sweet business, I warrant. What, 'tis no Westminster Hall business? Would you have my advice?

FREEMAN.
No, faith, 'tis a little Westminster Abbey business: I would have your consent.

WIDOW.
O fie, fie, sir, to me such discourse before my dear minor there!

JERRY.
Ay, ay, mother, he would be taking livery and seisin of your jointure by digging the turf, but I'll watch your waters, bully, ifac, Come away, mother.

Exit Jerry, haling away his mother.
Enter Fidelia.

FIDELIA.
Dear sir, you have pity. Beget but some in our captain for me.

FREEMAN.
Where is he?

FIDELIA.
Within, swearing as much as he did in the great storm and cursing you and sometimes sinks into calms and sighs and talks of his Olivia.

FREEMAN.
He would never trust me to see her. Is she handsome?

FIDELIA.
No, if you'll take my word, but I am not a proper judge.

FREEMAN.
What is she?

WIDOW.
A gentlewoman, I suppose, but of as mean a fortune as beauty, but her relations would not suffer her to go with him to the Indies, and his aversion to this side of the world, together with the late opportunity of commanding the convoy, would not let him stay here longer, though to enjoy her.

FREEMAN.
He loves her mightily then.

FIDELIA.
Yes, so well that the remainder of his fortune (I hear about five or six thousand pounds) he has left her in case he had died by the way or before she could prevail with her friends to follow him, which he expected she should do, [and has left behind him his great bosom friend to be her convoy to him.]

FREEMAN.
What charms has she for him if she be not handsome?

FIDELIA.
He fancies her, I suppose, the only woman of truth and sincerity in the world.

FREEMAN.
No common beauty I confess.

FIDELIA.
Or else sure he would not have trusted her with so great a share of his fortune in his absence; I suppose (since his late loss) all he has.

FREEMAN.
Why, has he left it in her own custody?

FIDELIA.
I am told so.

FREEMAN.

Then he has showed love to her indeed in leaving her, like an old husband that dies as soon as he has made his wife a good jointure. But I'll go in to him and speak for you and know more from him of his Olivia.

Exit.

FIDELIA.

His Olivia indeed, his happy Olivia,
Yet she was left behind, when I was with him;
But she was ne'er out of his mind or heart.
She has told him she loved him; I have showed it
And durst not tell him so till I had done,
Under this habit, such convincing acts
Of loving friendship for him that through it
He first might find out both my sex and love,
And, when I'd had him from his fair Olivia
And this bright world of artful beauties here,
Might then have hoped he would have looked on me
Amongst the sooty Indians; and I could,
To choose, there live his wife, where wives are forced
To live no longer when their husbands die,
Nay, what's yet worse, to share them whil'st they live
With many rival wives. But here he comes,
And I must yet keep out of his sight, not
To lose it forever.

Exit.

Enter Manly and Freeman.

FREEMAN.

But, pray, what strange charms has she that could make you love?

MANLY.

Strange charms indeed! She has beauty enough to call in question her wit or virtue, and her form would make a starved hermit a ravisher; yet her virtue and conduct would preserve her from the subtle lust of a pampered prelate. She is so perfect a beauty that art could not better it nor affectation deform it; yet all this is nothing. Her tongue, as well as face, ne'er knew artifice; nor ever did her words or looks contradict her heart. She is all truth and hates the lying, masking, daubing world as I do, for which I love her and for which I think she dislikes not me. For she has often shut out of her conversation for mine the gaudy, fluttering parrots of the town, apes and echoes of men only, and refused their commonplace pert chat, flattery and submissions, to be entertained with my sullen bluntness and honest love. And,

last of all, swore to me, since her parents would not suffer her to go with me, she would stay behind for no other man but follow me without their leave, if not to be obtained. Which oath –

FREEMAN.

Did you think she would keep?

MANLY.

Yes, for she is not (I tell you) like other women but can keep her promise, though she has sworn to keep it. But that she might the better keep it I left her the value of five or six thousand pound, for women's wants are generally their most importunate solicitors to love or marriage.

FREEMAN.

And money summons lovers more than beauty, and augments but their importunity and their number, so makes it the harder for a woman to deny 'em. For my part, I am for the French maxim; if you would have your female subjects loyal, keep 'em poor. But, in short, that your mistress may not marry, you have given her a portion.

MANLY.

She had given me her heart first and I am satisfied with the security; I can never doubt her truth and constancy.

FREEMAN.

It seems you do since you are fain to bribe it with money. But how come you to be so diffident of the man that says he loves you and not doubt the woman that says it?

MANLY.

I should, I confess, doubt the love of any other woman but her, as I do the friendship of any other man but him I have trusted, but I have such proofs of their faith as cannot deceive me.

FREEMAN.

Cannot!

MANLY.

Not but I know that generally no man can be a great enemy but under the name of friend; and if you are a cuckold, it is your friend only that makes you so, for your enemy is not admitted to your house; [if you are cheated in your fortune, 'tis your friend that does it, for your enemy is not made your trustee;] if your honour or good name be injured, 'tis your friend that does it still, because your enemy is not believed against you. Therefore I rather choose to go where honest downright barbarity is professed, where men devour one another like generous hungry lions [and tigers,] not like crocodiles, where they think the devil white, of our complexion, and I am already so far an Indian. But if your weak faith doubts this miracle of a woman, come along with me and believe and thou wilt find her so handsome that thou, who art so much my friend, wilt have a mind to lie with her and so will not fail to discover what her faith and thine is to me.

When we're in love the great adversity,
Our friends and mistresses at once we try.

ACT TWO

Scene One

Olivia's lodging. Enter Olivia, Eliza, Lettice.

OLIVIA.
Ah, cousin, what a world 'tis we live in! I am so weary of it.

ELIZA.
Truly, cousin, I can find no fault with it but that we cannot always live in't, for I can never be weary of it.

OLIVIA.
O hideous! You cannot be in earnest, sure, when you say you like the filthy world.

ELIZA.
You cannot be in earnest, sure, when you say you dislike it.

OLIVIA.
You are a very censorious creature, I find.

ELIZA.
I must confess I think we women as often discover where we love by railing, as men when they lie by their swearing, and the world is but a constant keeping gallant, whom we fail not to quarrel with when anything crosses us, yet cannot part with't for our hearts.

LETTICE.
A gallant indeed, madam, whom ladies first make jealous and then quarrel with it for being so, for if, by her indiscretion, a lady be talked of for a man, she cries presently, ''Tis a censorious world'; if by her vanity the intrigue be found out, ''Tis a prying, malicious world'; if by her over-fondness the gallant proves unconstant, ''Tis a false world'; and if by her niggardliness the chambermaid tells, ''Tis a perfidious world' – but that, I'm sure, your ladyship cannot say of the world yet, as bad as 'tis.

OLIVIA.
But I may say, ''Tis a very impertinent world.' Hold your peace. And, cousin, if the world be a gallant, 'tis such an one as is my aversion. Pray name it no more.

ELIZA.
But is it possible the world, which has such variety of charms for other women, can have none for you? Let's see – first, what d'ye think of dressing and fine clothes?

OLIVIA.

Dressing! Fie, fie, 'tis my aversion. But come hither, you
dowdy, methinks you might have opened this toure better. O
hideous! I cannot suffer it! D'ye see how't sits?

ELIZA.

Well enough, cousin, if dressing be your aversion.

OLIVIA.

'Tis so, and for variety of rich clothes, they are more my
aversion.

LETTICE.

Ay, 'tis because your ladyship wears 'em too long, for indeed a
gown, like a gallant, grows one's aversion by having too much
of it.

OLIVIA.

Insatiable creature! I'll be sworn I have had this not above
three days, cousin, and within this month have made some six
more.

ELIZA.

Then your aversion to 'em is not altogether so great.

OLIVIA.

Alas! 'Tis for my woman only I wear 'em, cousin.

LETTICE.

If it be for me only, madam, pray do not wear 'em.

ELIZA.

But what d'ye think of visits – balls –

OLIVIA.

O, I detest 'em.

ELIZA.

Of plays?

OLIVIA.

I abominate 'em: filthy, obscene, hideous things!

ELIZA.

What say you to masquerading in the winter and Hyde Park
in the summer?

OLIVIA.

Insipid pleasures I taste not.

ELIZA.

Nay, if you are for more solid pleasure, what think of you a
rich, young husband?

OLIVIA.

O horrid! Marriage! What a pleasure you have found out!
nauseate it of all things.

LETTICE.

But what does our ladyship think then of a liberal, handsom
young lover?

OLIVIA.

A handsome young fellow, you impudent! Be gone, out of my
sight. [Name a handsome young fellow to me!] Foh,
hideous, handsome young fellow I abominate. (*Spits.*)

ELIZA.

Indeed! But let's see – will nothing please you? What d'y
think of the court?

OLIVIA.

How? The court! The court, cousin! My aversion, m
aversion, my aversion of all aversions.

ELIZA.

How? The court! Where –

OLIVIA.

Where sincerity is a quality as out of fashion and a
unprosperous as bashfulness. [I could not laugh at a quibble
though it were a fat privy councillor's, nor praise a lord's il
verses, though I were myself the subject, nor an old lady'
young looks, though I were her woman, nor sit to a vai
young simile-maker, though he flattered me. In short,]
could not gloat upon a man when he comes into a room and
laugh at him when he goes out; I cannot rail at the absent t
flatter the standers-by; I –

ELIZA.

Well, but railing now is so common that 'tis no more malic
but the fashion, and the absent think they are no more th
worse for being railed at than the present think they are th
better for being flattered. And for the court –

OLIVIA.

Nay, do not defend the court, for you'll make me rail at it
like a trusting citizen's widow.

ELIZA.

Or like a Holborn lady, [who could not get into the last ball o
was out of countenance in the drawing-room the last Sunda
of her appearance there;] for none rail at the court but thos
who cannot get into it or else who are ridiculous when they ar
there, and I shall suspect you were laughed at when you wer
last there or would be a Maid of Honour.

OLIVIA.

I a Maid of Honour! To be a Maid of Honour were yet of all things my aversion.

ELIZA.

In what sense am I to understand you? But in fine by the word aversion I'm sure you dissemble, for I never knew woman yet that used it who did not. Come, [our tongues belie our hearts more than our pocket-glasses do our faces; but] methinks we ought to leave off dissembling, since 'tis grown of no use to us, for all wise observers understand us nowadays as they do dreams, [almanacs and Dutch gazettes,] by the contrary. And a man no more believes a woman when she says she has an aversion for him than when she says she'll cry out.

OLIVIA.

O filthy, hideous! Peace, cousin, or your discourse will be my aversion, and you may believe me.

ELIZA.

Yes, for if anything be a woman's aversion 'tis plain dealing from another woman and perhaps that's your quarrel to the world, for that will talk, as your woman says.

OLIVIA.

Talk not of me sure, for what men do I converse with? What visits do I admit?

Enter Boy.

BOY.

Here's the gentleman to wait upon you, madam.

OLIVIA.

On me! You little, unthinking fop, d'ye know what you say?

BOY.

Yes, madam, 'tis the gentleman that comes every day to you, who –

OLIVIA.

Hold your peace, you heedless little animal, and get you gone. This country boy, cousin, takes my dancing-master, tailor or the spruce milliner for visitors.

Exit Boy.

LETTICE.

No, madam, 'tis Mr Novel, I'm sure, by his talking so loud. I know his voice too, madam.

OLIVIA.

You know nothing, you buffle-headed, stupid creature you.

You would make my cousin believe I receive visits. But if it be Mr – what did you call him?.

LETTICE.

Mr Novel, madam, he that –

OLIVIA.

Hold your peace, I'll hear no more of him. But if it be your Mr – (I can't think of his name again) I suppose he has followed my cousin hither.

ELIZA.

No cousin, I will not rob you of the honour of the visit; 'tis to you, cousin, for I know him not.

OLIVIA.

Nor did I ever hear of him before, upon my honour, cousin. Besides, han't I told you that visits and the business of visits, flattery and detraction, are my aversion? D'ye think then I would admit such a coxcomb as he is, who rather than not rail will rail at the dead [whom none speak ill of,] and rather than not flatter will flatter the poets of the age, [whom none will flatter,] who affects novelty as much as the fashion and [is as fantastical as changeable and as well known as the fashion,] who likes nothing but what is new, nay, would choose to have his friend or his title a new one. In fine, he is my aversion.

ELIZA.

I find you do know him, cousin, at least have heard of him.

OLIVIA.

Yes, now I remember, I have heard of him.

ELIZA.

Well, but since he is such a coxcomb, for heaven's sake let him not come up. Tell him, Mrs Lettice, your lady is not within.

OLIVIA.

No, Lettice, tell him my cousin is here and that he may come up, for, notwithstanding I detest the sight of him, you may like his conversation and, though I would use him scurvily, I will not be rude to you in my own lodging. Since he has followed you hither, let him come up, I say.

ELIZA.

Very fine! Pray let him go to the devil, I say, for me. I know him not nor desire it. Send him away, Mrs Lettice.

OLIVIA.

Upon my word, she shan't. I must disobey your commands, to comply with your desires. Call him up, Lettice.

ELIZA.
Nay, I'll swear she shall not stir on that errand.

(*Holds Lettice.*)

OLIVIA.
Well then, I'll call him myself for you since you will have it so. (*Calls out at the door.*) Mr Novel, sir, sir.

Enter Novel.

NOVEL.
Madam, I beg your pardon; perhaps you were busy. I did not think you had company with you.

ELIZA (*aside*).
Yet he comes to me, cousin!

OLIVIA.
– Chairs there.

They sit.

Exit Lettice.

NOVEL.
Well, but, madam, d'ye know whence I come now?

OLIVIA.
From some melancholy place I warrant, sir, since they have lost your good company.

ELIZA.
So.

NOVEL.
From a place where they have treated me, at dinner, with so much civility and kindness, a pox on 'em, that I could hardly get away to you, dear madam.

OLIVIA.
You have a way with you so new and obliging, sir.

ELIZA (*apart to Olivia*).
You hate flattery, cousin!

NOVEL.
Nay, faith, madam, d'ye think my way new? Then you are obliging, madam. I must confess I hate imitation, to do anything like other people; all that know me do me the honour to say I am an original, faith. But, as I was saying, madam, I have been treated today with all the ceremony and kindness imaginable at my Lady Autum's, but the nauseous old woman at the upper end of her table-

OLIVIA.
Revives the old Grecian custom of serving in a death's head with their banquets.

NOVEL.
Hah, ha! Fine, just, i'faith, nay, and new. 'Tis like eating with the ghost in 'The Libertine'; she would frighten a man from her dinner with her hollow invitations and spoil one's stomach –

OLIVIA.
To meat or women. I detest her hollow cherry cheeks; she looks like an old coach new painted, affecting an unseemly smugness whilst she is ready to drop in pieces.

ELIZA (*apart to Olivia*).
You hate detraction I see, cousin!

NOVEL.
But the silly old fury, whilst she affects to look like a woman of this age, talks –

OLIVIA.
Like one of the last, and as passionately as an old courtier who has outlived his office.

NOVEL.
Yes, madam, but pray let me give you her character. Then, she never counts her age by the years but –

OLIVIA.
By the masques she has lived to see.

NOVEL.
Nay then, madam, I see you think a little harmless railing too great a pleasure for any but yourself and therefore I've done.

OLIVIA.
Nay, faith, you shall tell me who you had there at dinner.

NOVEL.
If you would hear me, madam.

OLIVIA.
Most patiently. Speak, sir.

NOVEL.
Then, we had her daughter –

OLIVIA.
Ay, her daughter, the very disgrace to good clothes, which she always wears but to heighten her deformity, not mend it, for she is still most spendidly, gallantly ugly and looks like an ill piece of daubing in a rich frame.

NOVEL.

So! But have you done with her, madam? And can you spare her to me a little now?

OLIVIA.

Ay, ay, sir.

NOVEL.

Then, she [is like –]

[OLIVIA.

She is, you'd say, like a city bride, the greater fortune but not the greater beauty for her dress.

NOVEL.

Well, yet have you done, madam? Then, she –]

OLIVIA.

[Then she] bestows as unfortunately on her face all the graces in fashion, as the languishing eye, the hanging or pouting lip; but as the fool is never more provoking than when he aims at wit, the ill-favoured of our sex are never more nauseous than when they would be beauties, adding to their natural deformity the artificial ugliness of affectation.

ELIZA.

So, cousin, I find one may have a collection of all one's acquaintances' pictures as well at your house as at Mr Lely's. Only the difference is, there we find 'em much handsomer than they are and like; here, much uglier and like. And you are the first of the profession of picture-drawing I ever knew without flattery.

OLIVIA.

I draw after the life, do nobody wrong, cousin.

ELIZA.

No, you hate flattery and detraction!

OLIVIA.

But, Mr Novel, who had you besides at dinner?

NOVEL.

Nay, the devil take me if I tell you, unless you will allow me the privilege of railing in my turn; but, now I think on't, the women ought to be your province, as the men are mine. And you must know, we had him whom –

OLIVIA.

Him whom –

NOVEL.

What? Invading me already? And giving the character before you know the man?

ELIZA.

No, that is not fair, though it be usual.

OLIVIA.

I beg your pardon, Mr Novel. Pray, go on.

NOVEL.

Then, I say, we had that familiar coxcomb, who is at home wheresoe'er he comes.

OLIVIA.

Ay, that fool –

NOVEL.

Nay then, madam, your servant. I'm gone. Taking a fool out of one's mouth is worse than taking the bread out of one's mouth.

OLIVIA.

I've done. Your pardon, Mr Novel, pray proceed.

NOVEL.

I say, the rogue, that he may be the only wit in the company, will let nobody else talk and –

OLIVIA.

Ay, those fops who love to talk all themselves are of all things my aversion.

NOVEL.

Then you'll let me speak, madam, sure. The rogue, I say, will force his jest upon you, and I hate a jest that's forced upon a man as much as a glass.

ELIZA.

Why, I hope, sir, he does not expect a man of your temperance in jesting should do him reason?

NOVEL.

What, interruption from this side too! I must then –

Offers to rise; Olivia holds him.

OLIVIA.

No, sir – You must know, cousin, that fop he means, though he talks only to be commended, will not give you leave to do't.

NOVEL.

But, madam –

OLIVIA.

He a wit! Hang him, he's only an adopter of straggling jests and fatherless lampoons, by the credit of which he eats at good tables [and so, like the barren beggar-woman, lives by borrowed children.]

[NOVEL.

Madam –

OLIVIA.

And never was author of anything but his news, but that is still all his own.]

NOVEL.

Madam, pray –

OLIVIA.

An eternal babbler, [and makes no more use of his ears than a man that sits at a play by his mistress or in fop-corner.] He's, in fine, a base, detracting fellow, and is my aversion. But who else prithee, Mr Novel, was there with you? Nay, you shan't stir.

NOVEL.

I beg your pardon, madam, I cannot stay in any place where I'm not allowed a little Christian liberty of railing.

OLIVIA.

Nay, prithee, Mr Novel, stay, and, though you should rail at me, I would hear you with patience. Prithee, who else was there with you?

NOVEL.

Your servant, madam.

OLIVIA.

Nay, prithee tell us, Mr Novel, prithee do.

NOVEL.

We had nobody else.

OLIVIA.

Nay, faith I know you had. Come, my Lord Plausible was there too, who is, cousin, a –

ELIZA.

You need not tell me what he is, cousin, for I know him to be a civil, good-natured, harmless gentleman, that speaks well of all the world and is always in good humour and –

OLIVIA.

Hold, cousin, hold. I hate detraction, but I must tell you, cousin, his civility is cowardice, his good nature want of wit, and has neither courage or sense to rail. And for his being always in humour, 'tis because he is never dissatisfied with himself. In fine he is my aversion, and I never admit his visits beyond my hall.

NOVEL.

No, he visit you! Damn him, cringing, grinning rogue. If I should see him coming up to you, I would make bold to kick him down again. Ha!–

Enter My Lord Plausible.

My dear lord, your most humble servant. *(Rises and salutes Plausible and kisses him.)*

ELIZA *(aside).*

So! I find kissing and railing succeed each other with the angry men as well as with the angry women, [and their quarrels are like love-quarrels, since absence is the only cause of them, for, as soon as the man appears again, they are over.]

LORD PLAUSIBLE.

Your most faithful, humble servant, generous Mr Novel, and madam, I am your eternal slave and kiss your fair hands, which I had done sooner, according to your commands, but –

OLIVIA.

No excuses, my lord.

ELIZA *(apart).*

What, you sent for him then, cousin?

NOVEL *(aside).*

Ha! Invited!

OLIVIA.

I know you must divide yourself, for your good company is too general a good to be engrossed by any particular friend.

LORD PLAUSIBLE.

O Lord, madam, my company! Your most obliged, faithful humble servant, but I could have brought you good company indeed, for I parted at your door with two of the worthiest bravest men –

OLIVIA.

Who were they, my lord?

NOVEL.

Who do you call the worthiest, bravest men, pray?

LORD PLAUSIBLE.

O the wisest, bravest gentlemen! Men of such honour and virtue! Of such good qualities! Ah –

[ELIZA *(aside).*

This is a coxcomb that speaks ill of all people a different way and libels everybody with dull praise and commonly in the wrong place, so makes his panegyrics abusive lampoons.]

OLIVIA.
But pray let me know who they were.

LORD PLAUSIBLE.
Ah! Such patterns of heroic virtue! Such –

NOVEL.
Well, but who the devil were they?

LORD PLAUSIBLE.
The honour of our nation, the glory of our age. Ah! I could dwell a twelvemonth on their praise, which indeed I might spare by telling their names: Sir John Current and Sir Richard Court-Title.

NOVEL.
Court-Title! Hah, ha.

OLIVIA.
And Sir John Current! Why will you keep such a wretch company, my lord?

LORD PLAUSIBLE.
Oh, madam, seriously you are a little too severe, for he is a man of unquestioned reputation in everything.

OLIVIA.
Yes, because he endeavours only with the women to pass for a man of courage [and with the bullies for a wit, with the wits for a man of business and with the men of business for a favourite at court and at court for good city security.]

NOVEL.
And for Sir Richard, he –

LORD PLAUSIBLE.
He loves your choice, picked company, persons that –

OLIVIA.
He loves a lord indeed, but –

NOVEL.
Pray, dear madam, let me have but a bold stroke or two at his picture. He loves a lord, as you say, though –

OLIVIA.
Though he borrowed his money and ne'er paid him again.

[NOVEL.
And would bespeak a place three days before at the back end of a lord's coach to Hyde Park.]

LORD PLAUSIBLE.
Nay, i'faith, i'faith, you are both too severe.

OLIVIA.
Then, to show yet more his passion for quality, he makes love to that fulsome coach-load of honour my Lady Goodly, for he is always at her lodging.

LORD PLAUSIBLE.
Because it is [the conventicle-gallant,] the meeting-house of all the fair ladies and glorious, superfine beauties of the town.

NOVEL.
Very fine ladies! There's first –

OLIVIA.
Her honour, as fat as an hostess.

LORD PLAUSIBLE.
She is something plump indeed, a goodly, comely, graceful person.

NOVEL.
Then there's my Lady Frances What-d'ye-call-'er? As ugly –

OLIVIA.
As a citizen's lawfully begotten daughter.

LORD PLAUSIBLE.
She has wit in abundance and the handsomest heel, elbow and tip of an ear you ever saw.

NOVEL.
Heel and elbow! Hah, ha! And there's my Lady Betty you know –

OLIVIA.
As sluttish and slatternly as an Irishwoman bred in France.

LORD PLAUSIBLE.
Ah, all she has hangs with a loose air indeed and becoming negligence.

ELIZA.
You see all faults with lover's eyes, I find, my lord.

LORD PLAUSIBLE.
Ah, madam, your most obliged, faithful, humble servant to command! [But you can say nothing sure against the superfine mistress –

OLIVIA.

I know who you mean. She is as censorious and detracting a jade as a superannuated sinner.

LORD PLAUSIBLE.

She has a smart way of raillery, 'tis confessed.]

NOVEL.

And then, for Mrs Grideline.

LORD PLAUSIBLE.

She I'm sure is –

OLIVIA.

One that never spoke ill of anybody, 'tis confessed, for she is as silent in conversation as a country lover and no better company than a clock [or a weather-glass,] for if she sounds 'tis but once an hour to put you in mind of the time of day [or to tell you 'twill be cold or hot, rain or snow.]

LORD PLAUSIBLE.

Ah, poor creature! She's extremely good and modest.

[NOVEL.

And for Mrs Bridlechin, she's –

OLIVIA.

As proud as a churchman's wife.

LORD PLAUSIBLE.

She's a woman of great spirit and honour and will not make herself cheap, 'tis true.]

NOVEL.

Then Mrs Hoyden, that calls all people by their surnames and is –

OLIVIA.

As familiar a duck –

NOVEL.

As an actress in the tiring-room. There I was once beforehand with you, madam.

LORD PLAUSIBLE.

Mrs Hoyden! A poor, affable, good-natured soul! But the divine Mrs Trifle comes thither too; sure her beauty, virtue and conduct you can say nothing to.

OLIVIA.

No!

NOVEL.

No! – Pray let me speak, madam.

OLIVIA.

First, can anyone be called beautiful that squints?

LORD PLAUSIBLE.

Her eyes languish a little, I own.

NOVEL.

Languish! Hah, ha.

OLIVIA.

Languish! Then for her conduct she was seen at 'The Country Wife' after the first day. There's for you, my lord.

LORD PLAUSIBLE.

But, madam, she was not seen to use her fan all the play long, turn aside her head, or by a conscious blush discover more guilt than modesty.

OLIVIA.

Very fine! Then you think a woman modest that sees the hideous 'Country Wife' without blushing or publishing her detestation of it? D'ye hear him, cousin?

ELIZA.

Yes, and am, I must confess, something of his opinion and think that as an over-conscious fool at a play, by endeavouring to show the author's want of wit, exposes his own to more censure, so may a lady call her modesty in question by publicly cavilling with the poets, for all those grimaces of honour and artificial modesty disparage a woman's real virtue as much as the use of white and red does the natural complexion, and you must use very, very little if you would have it thought your own.

[OLIVIA.

Then you would have a woman of honour with passive looks, ears and tongue undergo all the hideous obscenity she hears at nasty plays?

ELIZA.

Truly, I think a woman betrays her want of modesty by showing it publicly in a playhouse as much as a man does his want of courage by a quarrel there, for the truly modest and stout say least and are least exceptious, especially in public.]

OLIVIA.

O hideous! Cousin, this cannot be your opinion, but you are one of those who have the confidence to pardon the filthy play.

ELIZA.

Why, what is there of ill in't, say you?

OLIVIA.

O fie, fie, fie, would you put me to the blush anew? Call all the blood into my face again? But to satisfy you then, first, the clandestine obscenity in the very name of Horner.

ELIZA.

Truly, 'tis so hidden I cannot find it out, I confess.

OLIVIA.

O horrid! Does it not give you the rank conception or image of a goat, a town-bull or a satyr? Nay, what is yet a filthier image than all the rest, that of an eunuch?

ELIZA.

What then? I can think of a goat, a bull or satyr without any hurt.

OLIVIA.

Ay, but, cousin, one cannot stop there.

ELIZA.

I can, cousin.

OLIVIA.

O no, for when you have those filthy creatures in your head once, the next thing you think is what they do, as their defiling of honest men's beds and couches, rapes upon sleeping and waking country virgins under hedges and on haycocks. Nay, farther –

ELIZA.

Nay, no farther, cousin. We have enough of your comment on the play, which will make me more ashamed than the play itself.

OLIVIA.

O, believe me, 'tis a filthy play, and you may take my word for a filthy play as soon as another's, but the filthiest thing in that play, or any other play, is –

ELIZA.

Pray keep it to yourself, if it be so.

OLIVIA.

No, faith, you shall know it. I'm resolved to make you out of love with the play. I say, the lewdest, filthiest thing is his china; nay, I will never forgive the beastly author his china. He has quite taken away the reputation of poor china itself and sullied the most innocent and pretty furniture of a lady's chamber, insomuch that I was fain to break all my defiled vessels. You see I have none left; nor you, I hope.

ELIZA.

You'll pardon me, I cannot think the worse of my china for that of the playhouse.

OLIVIA.

Why, you will not keep any now sure! 'Tis now as unfit an ornament for a lady's chamber as the pictures that come from Italy and other hot countries, as appears by their nudities, which I always cover or scratch out, wheresoe'er I find 'em. But china! Out upon't, filthy china, nasty, debauched china!

ELIZA.

All this will not put me out of conceit with china nor the play, which is acted today or another of the same beastly author's, as you call him, which I'll go see.

OLIVIA.

You will not, sure! Nay, you sha'not venture your reputation by going and mine by leaving me alone with two men here. Nay, you'll disoblige me for ever, if – (*Pulls her back.*)

ELIZA.

I stay! – your servant.

Exit Eliza.

OLIVIA.

Well – but my lord, though you justify everybody, you cannot in earnest uphold so beastly a writer, whose ink is so smutty, as one may say.

LORD PLAUSIBLE.

Faith, I dare swear the poor man did not think to disoblige the ladies by any amorous, soft, passionate, luscious saying in his play.

OLIVIA.

Foy, my lord, but what think you, Mr Novel, of the play? Though I know you are a friend to all that are new.

NOVEL.

Faith, madam, I must confess the new plays would not be the worse for my advice but I could never get the silly rogues, the poets, to mind what I say: but I'll tell you what counsel I gave the surly fool you speak of.

OLIVIA.

What was't?

NOVEL.

Faith, to put his play into rithme, for rithme, you know, often makes mystical nonsense pass with the critics for wit and a double-meaning saying with the ladies for soft, tender and moving passion. But, now I talk of passion. I saw your old lover this morning – Captain (*Whispers.*)

Enter Captain Manly, Freeman and Fidelia standing behind.

OLIVIA.
Whom? – Nay, you need not whisper.

MANLY.
We are luckily got hither unobserved. – How! In a close conversation with these supple rascals, [the outcasts of sempstresses' shops?]

FREEMAN.
Faith, pardon her, captain, that, since she could no longer be entertained with your manly bluntness and honest love, she takes up with the pert chat and commonplace flattery of these fluttering parrots of the town, apes and echoes of men only.

MANLY.
Do not you, sir, play the echo [too, mock me,] dally with my own words and show yourself as impertinent as they are.

FREEMAN.
Nay, captain –

FIDELIA.
Nay, lieutenant, do not excuse her. Methinks she looks very kindly upon 'em both and seems to be pleased with what that fool there says to her.

MANLY.
You lie, sir, and hold your peace that I may not be provoked to give you a worse reply.

OLIVIA.
Manly returned, d'ye say! And is he safe?

NOVEL.
My lord saw him too. (*Whisper to Plausible.*) Hark you, my lord.

MANLY (*aside*).
She yet seems concerned for my safety and perhaps they are admitted now here but for their news of me, [for intelligence indeed is the common passport of nauseous fools when they go their round of good tables and houses.]

OLIVIA.
I heard of his fighting only, without particulars, and confess I always loved his brutal courage because it made me hope it might rid me of his more brutal love.

MANLY (*apart*).
What's that?

OLIVIA.
But is he at last returned, d'ye say, unhurt?

NOVEL.
Ay faith, without doing his business, for the rogue has been these two years pretending to a wooden leg, which he would take from fortune as kindly as the staff of a marshal of France [and rather read his name in a gazette –]

[OLIVIA.
Than in the entail of a good estate.]

MANLY (*aside*)
So!

NOVEL.
I have an ambition, I must confess, of losing my heart before such a fair enemy as yourself, madam, but that silly rogues should be ambitious of losing their arms and –

OLIVIA.
Looking like a pair of compasses.

NOVEL.
But he has no use of his arms but to set them on kimbow, for he never pulls off his hat, at least not to me, I'm sure, for you must know, madam, he has a fanatical hatred to good company: he can't abide me.

LORD PLAUSIBLE.
O, be not so severe to him as to say he hates good company, for I assure you he has a great respect, esteem and kindness for me.

[MANLY (*aside*).
That kind, civil rogue has spoken yet ten thousand times worse of me than t'other.]

OLIVIA.
Well, if he be returned, Mr Novel, then shall I be pestered again with his boisterous sea love, have my alcove smell like a cabin, my chamber perfumed with his tarpaulin Brandenburgh, and hear vollies of brandy sighs, enough to make a fog in one's room. Foh! I hate a lover that smells like Thames Street!

MANLY (*aside*).
I can bear no longer and need hear no more. – But, since you have these two pulvillio boxes, these essence bottles, this pair of musk-cats here, I hope I may venture to come yet nearer you.

OLIVIA.
Overheard us then?

NOVEL (*aside*).
I hope he heard me not.

LORD PLAUSIBLE.
Most noble and heroic captain, your most obliged, faithful,
humble servant.

NOVEL.
Dear tar, thy humble servant.

MANLY.
Away – madam. (*Thrusts Novel and Plausible on each side.*)

OLIVIA.
Nay, I think I have fitted you for listening.

MANLY.
You have fitted me for believing you could not be fickle
though you were young, could not dissemble love though
'twas your interest, [nor be vain though you were handsome,]
nor break your promise though to a parting lover, [nor abuse
your best friend though you had wit.] But I take not your
contempt of me worse than your esteem or civility for these
things here though you know 'em.

NOVEL.
Things!

LORD PLAUSIBLE.
Let the captain rally a little.

MANLY.
Yes, things. Can'st thou be angry, thou thing? (*Coming up to
Novel.*)

NOVEL.
No, since my lord says you speak in raillery, for, though your
sea-raillery be something rough, yet I confess we use one
another to as bad every day at Locket's and never quarrel for
the matter.

LORD PLAUSIBLE.
Nay, noble captain, be not angry with him. A word with you,
I beseech you – (*Whispers to Manly.*)

OLIVIA (*aside*).
Well, we women, like the rest of the cheats of the world, when
our cullies [or creditors] have found us out and will [or can]
trust no longer, [pay debts and] satisfy obligations with a
quarrel, [the kindest present a man can make to his mistress
when he can make no more presents,] for oftentimes in love
as at cards we are forced to play foul, only to give over the
game, and use our lovers, like the cards, when we can get no
more by 'em, throw 'em up in a pet upon the first dispute.

MANLY.
My lord, all that you have made me know by your whispering,
which I knew not before, is that you have a stinking breath:
there's a secret for your secret.

LORD PLAUSIBLE.
Pshaw! Pshaw!

MANLY.
But, madam, tell me, pray, what was't about this spark could
take you? Was it the merit of his fashionable impudence, the
briskness of his noise, the wit of his laugh, [his judgement or
fancy in his garniture?] Or was it a well-trimmed glove or the
scent of it that charmed you?

NOVEL.
Very well, sir, Gad, these sea-captains make nothing of
dressing. But let me tell you, sir, a man by his dress, as much
as by anything, shows his wit and judgement, nay, and his
courage too.

FREEMAN.
How his courage, Mr Novel?

NOVEL.
Why, for example, by red breeches, tucked-up hair or
peruke, a greasy broad belt and nowadays a short sword.

MANLY.
Thy courage will appear more by thy belt than thy sword, I
dare swear. Then, madam, for this gentle piece of courtesy,
this man of tame honour, what could you find in him? Was it
his languishing affected tone? His mannerly look? [His
second-hand flattery, the refuse of the playhouse tiring-
rooms? Or his slavish obsequiousness in watching at the door
of your box at the playhouse for your hand to your chair?] Or
his janty way of playing with your fan? Or was it the
gunpowder spot on his hand or the jewel in his ear that
purchased your heart?

OLIVIA.
Good jealous captain, no more of your –

LORD PLAUSIBLE.
No, let him go on, madam, for perhaps he may make you
laugh, and I would contribute to your pleasure any way.

MANLY.
Gentle rogue!

OLIVIA.
No, noble captain, you cannot sure think anything could take me more than that heroic title of yours, captain, for you know we women love honour inordinately.

NOVEL.
Hah, ha, faith, she is with thee, bully, for thy raillery.

MANLY (*aside to Novel*).
Faith, so shall I be with you, no bully, for your grinning.

OLIVIA.
Then, that noble lion-like mien of yours, that soldier-like, weather-beaten complexion and that manly rougliness of your voice, how can they otherwise than charm us women who hate effeminacy!

NOVEL.
Hah, ha! Faith, I can't hold from laughing.

MANLY (*aside to Novel*).
Nor shall I from kicking anon.

OLIVIA.
And then, that captain-like carelessness in your dress, but especially your scarf; 'twas just such another, only a little higher tied, made me in love with my tailor as he passed by my window the last training day, for we women adore a martial man, and you have nothing wanting to make you more one, or more agreeable, but a wooden leg.

LORD PLAUSIBLE.
Nay, i'faith there your ladyship was a wag, and it was fine, just and well rallied.

NOVEL.
Ay, ay, madam, with you ladies too, martial men must needs be very killing.

MANLY.
Peace, you Bartholomew-Fair buffoons, and be not you vain that these laugh on your side, for they will laugh at their own dull jests. But no more of 'em, for I will only suffer now this lady to be witty and merry.

OLIVIA.
You would not have your panegyric interrupted. I go on then to your humour. Is there anything more agreeable than the pretty sullenness of that? Than the greatness of your courage? – which most of all appears in your spirit of contradiction, for you dare give all mankind the lie and your opinion is your only mistress, for you renounce that too when it becomes another man's.

NOVEL.
Hah, ha! I cannot hold. I must laugh at thee, tar, faith!

LORD PLAUSIBLE.
And i'faith, dear captain, I beg your pardon and leave to laugh at you too, though I protest I mean you no hurt, but when a lady rallies, a stander-by must be complaisant and do her reason in laughing. Hah, ha.

MANLY.
Why, you impudent, pitiful wretches, you presume sure upon your effeminacy to urge me, for you are in all things so like women that you may think it in me a kind of cowardice to beat you.

OLIVIA.
No hectoring, good captain.

MANLY.
Or perhaps you think this lady's presence secures you. But have a care, she has talked herself out of all the respect I had for her, and [by using me ill before you has given me privilege of using you so before her. But] if you would [preserve your respect to her and] not be beaten before her, go, be gone immediately.

NOVEL.
Be gone! What?

LORD PLAUSIBLE.
Nay, worthy, noble, generous captain.

MANLY.
Be gone, I say.

NOVEL.
Be gone again! To us be gone!

MANLY.
No chattering, baboons, instantly be gone. Or –

Manly puts 'em out of the room: Novel struts, Plausible cringe

NOVEL.
Well, madam, we'll go make the cards ready in your bed chamber. Sure you will not stay long with him.

Exeunt Plausible, Nove

OLIVIA.
Turn hither your rage, good Captain Swaggerhuff, and b saucy with your mistress, like a true captain; but be civil your rivals and betters and do not threaten anything but m here, no, not so much as my windows, nor do not think you

self in the lodgings of one of your suburb mistresses beyond
the Tower.

MANLY.

Do not give me cause to think so, for those less infamous
women part with their lovers, just as you did from me, with
unforced vows of constancy and floods of willing tears, but the
same winds bear away their lovers and their vows; and for
their grief, if the credulous, unexpected fools return, they find
new comforters, fresh cullies, such as I found here. The
mercenary love of those women too suffers shipwreck with
their gallants' fortunes. Now you have heard chance has used
me scurvily, therefore you do too. Well, persevere in your
ingratitude, falsehood and disdain; have constancy in something and I promise you to be as just to your real scorn as I
was to your feigned love and henceforward will despise,
contemn, hate loathe and detest you, most faithfully.

Enter Lettice.

OLIVIA.

Get the ombre cards ready in the next room, Lettice, and –

Whispers to Lettice who goes out.

FREEMAN.

Bravely resolved, captain.

FIDELIA.

And you'll be sure to keep your word, I hope, sir.

MANLY.

I hope so too.

FIDELIA.

Do you but hope it, sir? If you are not as good as your word,
'twill be the first time you ever bragged, sure.

MANLY.

She has restored my reason with my heart.

FREEMAN.

But, now you talk of restoring, captain, there are other things
which, next to one's heart, one would not part with: I mean
your jewels and money, which it seems she has, sir.

MANLY.

What's that to you, sir?

FREEMAN.

Pardon me, whatsoever is yours, I have a share in't, I'm sure,
which I will not lose for asking, though you may be too
generous, or too angry now to do't yourself.

FIDELIA.

Nay, then I'll make bold to make my claim too.

Both going towards Olivia.

MANLY.

Hold, you impertinent, officious fops. (*Aside.*) How have I
been deceived!

FREEMAN.

Madam, there are certain appurtenances to a lover's heart,
called jewels, which always go along with it.

FIDELIA.

And which, with lovers, have no value in themselves but from
the heart they come with; our captain's, madam, it seems you
scorn to keep and much more will those worthless things
without it, I am confident.

OLIVIA.

A gentleman so well made as you are may be confident – us
easy women could not deny you anything you ask, if 'twere
for yourself; but, since 'tis for another, I beg your leave to
give him my answer. (*Aside.*) An agreeable young fellow this!
– And would not be my aversion! (*Aside to Manly.*) Captain,
your young friend here has a very persuading face, I confess;
yet you might have asked me yourself for those trifles you left
with me, which (hark you a little, for I dare trust you with the
secret; you are a man of so much honour, I'm sure), I say
then, not expecting your return, or hoping ever to see you
again, I have delivered your jewels to –

MANLY.

Whom?

OLIVIA.

My husband!

MANLY.

Your husband!

OLIVIA.

Ay, my husband, for, since you could leave me, I am lately
and privately married to one who is a man of so much honour
and experience in the world that I dare not ask him for your
jewels again to restore 'em to you, lest he should conclude you
never would have parted with 'em to me, on any other score
but the exchange of my honour, which rather than you'd let
me lose, you'd lose, I'm sure, yourself those trifles of yours.

MANLY.

Triumphant impudence! But married too!

OLIVIA.

O, speak not so loud; my servants know it not. I am married; there's no resisting one's destiny, or love, you know.

MANLY.

Why, did you love him too?

OLIVIA.

Most passionately, nay, love him now, though I have married him, and he me; which mutual love, I hope, you are too good, too generous a man to disturb by any future claim or visits to me. 'Tis true he is now absent in the country but returns shortly. Therefore, I beg of you, for your own ease and quiet, and my honour, you will never see me more.

MANLY.

I wish I never had seen you.

OLIVIA.

But if you should ever have anything to say to me hereafter, let that young gentleman there be your messenger.

MANLY.

You would be kinder to him; I find he should be welcome.

OLIVIA.

Alas, his youth would keep my husband from suspicions and his visits from scandal, for we women may have pity for such as he but no love. And I already think you do not well to spirit him away to sea, and the sea is already but too rich with the spoils of the shore.

MANLY (aside).

True perfect woman! If I could say anything more injurious to her now, I would, for I could out-rail a bilked whore or a kicked coward, but, now I think on't, that were rather to discover my love than hatred, and I must not talk, for something I must do.

OLIVIA (aside).

I think I have given him enough of me now never to be troubled with him again.

Enter Lettice.

Well, Lettice, are the cards and all ready within? I come then. Captain, I beg your pardon; you will not make one at ombre?

MANLY.

No, madam, but I'll wish you a little good luck before you go.

OLIVIA.

No, if you would have me thrive, curse me, for that you'll d heartily, I suppose.

MANLY.

Then, if you will have it so, may all the curses light upon yo women ought to fear and you deserve: first, may the curse c loving play attend your sordid covetousness and fortune chea you by trusting to her as you have cheated me; the curse c pride or a good reputation fall on your lust; the curse c affectation on your beauty; the curse of your husband' company on your pleasures; and the curse of your gallant' disappointments in his absence; and the curse of scorn jealousy or despair on your love – and then the curse of lovin on.

OLIVIA.

And, to requite all your curses, I will only return you you last. May the curse of loving me still fall upon your prou hard heart that could be so cruel to me in these horrid curse but heaven forgive you.

Exit Olivi

MANLY.

Hell and the devil reward thee.

FREEMAN.

Well, you see now mistresses, like friends, are lost by lettin 'em handle your money, and most women are such kind c witches, who can have no power over a man unless you giv 'em money; but when once they have got any fro you, they never leave you, till they have all; therefore I nev dare give a woman a farthing.

[MANLY.

Well, there is yet this comfort by losing one's money wi one's mistress: a man is out of danger of getting another, being made prize again by love, who, like a pirate, takes yc by spreading false colours, but when once you have run yo ship aground, the treacherous picaroon loofs, so by your ru you save yourself from slavery at least.]

Enter Boy.

BOY.

Mrs Lettice, here's Madam Blackacre come to wait upon h honour.

Exeunt Boy and Letti

MANLY.

D'ye hear that? Let us be gone before she comes, f

henceforward I'll avoid the whole damned sex forever and woman as a sinking ship.

Exeunt Manly and Fidelia.

FREEMAN.
And I'll stay to revenge on her your quarrel to the sex, for out of love to her jointure and hatred to business I would marry her, to make an end of her thousand suits and my thousand engagements, to the comfort of two unfortunate sorts of people: my plaintiffs and her defendants, my creditors and her adversaries.

Enter Widow Blackacre led in by Major Oldfox, and Jerry Blackacre following, laden with green bags.

WIDOW.
'Tis an arrant sea-ruffian, but I am glad I met with him [at last] to serve him again, major, for the last service was not good in law. Boy, duck, Jerry, where is my paper of memorandums? Give me, child. So. Where is my cousin Olivia now, my kind relation?

FREEMAN.
Here is one that would be your kind relation, madam.

WIDOW.
What mean you, sir?

FREEMAN.
Why, faith (to be short) to marry you, widow.

WIDOW.
Is not this the wild, rude person we saw at Captain Manly's?

JERRY.
Ay, forsooth, an't please.

WIDOW.
What would you? What are you? Marry me!

FREEMAN.
Ay, faith, for I am a younger brother and you are a widow.

WIDOW.
You are an impertinent person, and go about your business.

FREEMAN.
I have none but to marry thee, widow.

WIDOW.
But I have other business, I'd have you to know.

FREEMAN.
But you have no business anights, widow, and I'll make you

pleasanter business than any you have; for anights, I assure you, I am a man of great business, for the business –

WIDOW.
Go, I'm sure you're an idle fellow.

FREEMAN.
Try me but, widow, and employ me as you find my abilities and industry.

OLDFOX.
Pray be civil to the lady, Mr –. She's a person of quality, a person that is no person –

FREEMAN.
Yes, but she's a person that is a widow. Be you mannerly to her because you are to pretend only to be her squire, to arm her to her lawyer's chambers; but I will be impudent and bawdy, for she must love and marry me.

WIDOW.
Marry come up, you saucy familiar Jack! You think with us widows, 'tis no more than up and ride. Gad forgive me, nowadays every idle, young, hectoring, roaring companion with a pair of turned red breeches and a broad back thinks to carry away any widow of the best degree, but I'd have you to know, sir, all widows are not got, like places at court, by impudence and importunity only.

OLDFOX.
No, no, [soft, soft.] You are a young man and not fit –

FREEMAN.
For a widow? Yes, sure, old man, the fitter.

OLDFOX.
Go to, go to, if others had not laid in their claims before you –

FREEMAN.
Not you, I hope.

OLDFOX.
Why not I, sir? [Sure,] I am a much more proportionable match for her than you, sir, I, who am an elder brother, of a comfortable fortune and of equal years with her.

WIDOW.
How's that? You unmannerly person, I'd have you to know, I was born in *ann' undec' Caroli prim'*.

OLDFOX.
Your pardon, lady, your pardon. Be not offended with your [very] servant. – But I say, sir, you are a beggarly younger

brother, twenty years younger than her, without any land or stock but your great stock of impudence. Therefore what pretension can you have to her?

FREEMAN.

You have made it for me; first, because I am a younger brother.

WIDOW.

Why, is that a sufficient plea to a relict? How appears it, sir? By what foolish custom?

FREEMAN.

By custom time out of mind only. Then, sir, because I have nothing to keep me after her death, I am the likelier to take care of her life. And, for my being twenty years younger than her and having a sufficient stock of impudence, I leave it to her whether they will be valid exceptions to me in her widow's law or equity.

OLDFOX.

[Well, she has been so long in Chancery that I'll stand to her equity and decree between us.] Come, lady, pray snap up this young snap [at first] or we shall be troubled with him. Give him a city widow's answer (*Aside to the Widow.*) that is, with all the ill breeding imaginable. – Come, madam.

WIDOW.

Well then, to make an end of this foolish wooing, for nothing interrupts business more. First, for you, major –

OLDFOX.

You declare in my favour then?

FREEMAN.

What, direct the court? (*To Jerry.*) Come, young lawyer, thou shalt be a counsel for me.

JERRY.

Gad, I shall betray your cause then as well as an older lawyer, never stir.

WIDOW.

First, I say, for you, major, my walking hospital of an ancient foundation, thou bag of mummy that wouldst fall asunder if 'twere not for thy cerecloths –

OLDFOX.

How, lady?

FREEMAN.

Hah, ha –

JERRY.

Hey, brave mother! Use all suitors thus, for my sake.

WIDOW.

Thou withered, hobbling, distorted cripple; nay, thou art cripple all over. Wouldst thou make me the staff of thy age, the crutch of thy decrepitness? Me –

FREEMAN.

Well said, widow! Faith, thou wouldst make a man love thee now without dissembling.

WIDOW.

Thou senseless, impertinent, quibbling, drivelling, feeble, paralytic, impotent, fumbling, frigid nincompoop.

JERRY.

Hey, brave mother for calling of names, ifac!

WIDOW.

Wouldst thou make [a caudlemaker,] a nurse of me? Can't you be bedrid without a bedfellow? Won't your swanskins, furs, flannels [and the scorched trencher] keep you warm there? Would you have me your Scotch warming-pan, with a pox to you? Me! –

OLDFOX.

O heavens!

FREEMAN.

I told you I should be thought the fitter man, major.

JERRY.

Ay, you old fobus, and you would have been my guardian, would you? To have taken care of my estate, that half of't should never come to me, by letting long leases at peppercorn rents.

WIDOW.

If I would have married an old man, 'tis well known I might have married an earl, nay, what's more, a judge [and been covered the winter nights with the lambskins which I prefer to the ermines of nobles.] And dost thou think I would wrong my poor minor there for you?

FREEMAN.

Your minor is a chopping minor, God bless him. (*Strokes Jerry on the head.*)

OLDFOX.

Your minor may be a major of horse or foot for his bigness, and it seems you will have the cheating of your minor to yourself.

WIDOW.

Pray, sir, bear witness. Cheat my minor! I'll bring my action of the case for the slander.

FREEMAN.

Nay, I would bear false witness for thee now, widow, since you have done me justice and have thought me the fitter man for you.

WIDOW.

Fair and softly, sir. 'Tis my minor's case more than my own, and I must do him justice now on you.

FREEMAN.

How?

OLDFOX.

So then.

WIDOW.

You are first, I warrant, some renegado from the Inns of Court and the law, and thou'lt come to suffer for't by the law, that is, be hanged.

JERRY.

Not about your neck, forsooth, I hope.

FREEMAN.

But, madam –

OLDFOX.

Hear the court.

WIDOW.

Thou art some debauched, drunken, lewd, hectoring, gaming companion and want'st some widow's old gold to nick upon; but, I thank you sir, that's for my lawyers.

FREEMAN.

Faith, we should ne'er quarrel about that, for guineas would serve my turn. But, widow –

WIDOW.

Thou art a foul-mouthed boaster of thy lust, a mere braggadocio of thy strength for wine and women and wilt belie thyself more than thou dost women and art every way a base deceiver of women; and would deceive me too, would you?

FREEMAN.

Nay, faith, widow, this is judging without seeing the evidence.

WIDOW.

I say, you are a worn-out whoremaster at five and twenty both in body and fortune, and cannot be trusted by the common wenches of the town, lest you should not pay 'em, nor by the wives of the town, lest you should pay 'em; so you want women and would have me your bawd, to procure 'em for you.

FREEMAN.

Faith, if you had any good acquaintance, widow, 'twould be civilly done of thee, for I am just come from sea.

WIDOW.

I mean, you would have me keep you that you might turn keeper, for poor widows are only used like bawds by you; you go to church with us but to get other women to lie with. In fine, you are a cheating, chousing spendthrift and, having sold your own annuity, would waste my jointure.

JERRY.

And make havoc of our estate personal and all our old gilt plate. I should soon be picking up all our mortgaged apostle-spoons, bowls and beakers out of most of the alehouses betwixt Hercules' Pillars and the Boatswain in Wapping; nay, and you'd be scouring amongst my trees and make 'em knock down one another, like routed, reeling watchmen at midnight. Would you so, bully?

FREEMAN.

Nay, prithee, widow, hear me.

WIDOW.

No, sir. I'd have you to know, thou pitiful, paltry, lath-backed fellow, if I would have married a young man, 'tis well known I could have had any young heir in Norfolk, [nay, the hopefullest young man this day at the King's Bench Bar,] I that am a relict and executrix of known plentiful assets and parts, who understand myself and the law. And would you have me under covert baron again? No, sir, no covert baron for me.

FREEMAN.

But, dear widow, hear me. I value you only, not your jointure.

WIDOW.

Nay, sir, hold there. I know your love to a widow is covetousness of her jointure. And a widow a little stricken in years with a good jointure is like an old mansion house in a good purchase, never valued, but take one, take t'other. And perhaps when you are in possession you'd neglect it, let it drop to the ground for want of necessary repairs or expenses upon't.

FREEMAN.

No, widow, one would be sure to keep all tight when one is to forfeit one's lease by dilapidation.

WIDOW.

Fie, fie, I neglect my business with this foolish discourse of love. Jerry, child, let me see the list of the jury; I'm sure my cousin Olivia has some relations amongst 'em. But where is she?

FREEMAN.

Nay, widow, but hear me one world only.

WIDOW.

Nay, sir, no more, pray. I will no more hearken again to your foolish love motions than to offers of arbitration.

Exeunt Widow and Jerry.

FREEMAN.

Well, I'll follow thee yet, for he that has a pretension [at court or] to a widow must never give over for a little ill usage.

OLDFOX.

Therefore I'll get her by assiduity, patience and long-sufferings, which you will not undergo, for you idle young fellows leave off love when it comes to be business, and industry gets more women, than love.

FREEMAN.

Ay, industry, the fool's and old man's merit; but I'll be industrious too and make a business on't and get her by law, wrangling and contests and not by sufferings. And, because you are no dangerous rival, I'll give thee counsel, major:
If you litigious widow e'er would gain,
Sigh not to her but by the law complain;
To her, as to a bawd, defendant sue
With statutes and make justice pimp for you.

Exeunt.

ACT THREE

Scene One

Westminster Hall. Enter Manly and Freeman, two Sailors behind.

MANLY.

I hate this place, [worse than a man that has inherited a chancery suit.] I wish I were well out on't again.

FREEMAN.

Why, you need not be afraid of this place, for a man without money needs no more fear a crowd of lawyers, than a crowd of pickpockets.

MANLY.

This, the reverend of the law would have thought the palace [or residence] of justice; but, if it be, she lives here [with the state of a Turkish Emperor,] rarely seen, and besieged, rather than defended, by her numerous black guard here.

FREEMAN.

Methinks 'tis like one of their own halls in Christmas time, whither from all parts fools bring their money to try by the dice – not the worst judges – whether it shall be their own or no. [But after a tedious fretting and wrangling they drop away all their money on both sides and, finding neither the better, at last go emptily and lovingly away together to the tavern, joining their curses against the young lawyers' box, that sweeps all like the old ones.]

MANLY.

Spoken like a revelling Christmas lawyer.

FREEMAN.

Yes, I was one, I confess, but was fain to leave the law out of conscience and fall to making false musters, rather chose to cheat the king than his subjects, plunder rather than take fees.

MANLY.

Well, a plague and a purse famine light on the law, and that female limb of it who dragged me hither today. But prithee go see if in that crowd of daggled gowns there thou canst find her. (*Pointing to a crowd of lawyers at the end of the stage.*)

Exit Freeman

How hard it is to be an hypocrite!
At least to me, who am but newly so.
I thought it once a kind of knavery,
Nay, cowardice, to hide one's faults; but now

The common frailty, love, becomes my shame.
He must not know I love th'ungrateful still,
Lest he contemn me more than she, for I,
It seems, can undergo a woman's scorn
But not a man's –

Enter to him Fidelia.

IDELIA.
Sir, good sir, generous captain.

MANLY.
Prithee, kind impertinence, leave me. Why shouldst thou follow me, [flatter my generosity now,] since thou know'st I have no money left? If I had it, I'd give it thee, to buy my quiet.

IDELIA.
I never followed yet, sir, reward or fame but you alone, nor do I now beg anything but leave to share your miseries. You should not be a niggard of 'em, since methinks you have enough to spare. Let me follow you now because you hate me, as you have often said.

MANLY.
I ever hated a coward's company, I must confess.

IDELIA.
Let me follow you till I am none then, for you, I'm sure, will through such worlds of dangers that I shall be inured to 'em; nay, I shall be afraid of your anger more than danger and so turn valiant out of fear. Dear captain, do not cast me off till you have tried me once more. Do not, do not go to sea again without me.

MANLY.
Thou to sea! To court, thou fool. Remember the advice I gave thee; thou art a handsome spaniel and canst fawn naturally. Go, busk about and run thyself into the next great man's lobby; first fawn upon the slaves without and then run into the lady's bedchamber; thou may'st be admitted at last to tumble her bed. Go seek, I say, and lose me, for I am not able to keep thee; I have not bread for myself.

IDELIA.
Therefore I will not go, because then I may help and serve you.

MANLY.
Thou!

FIDELIA.
I warrant you, sir, for at worst I could beg or steal for you.

MANLY.
Nay, more bragging! Dost thou not know there's venturing your life in stealing? Go, prithee, away. Thou art as hard to shake off as that flattering effeminating mischief, love.

FIDELIA.
Love, did you name? Why you are not so miserable as to be yet in love, sure!

MANLY.
No, no, prithee away, be gone, on – (*Aside.*) I had almost discovered my love and shame. Well, if I had? That thing could not think the worst of me – or if he did? – No – yes, he shall know it – he shall – but then I must never leave him, for they are such secrets that make [parasites and] pimps lords of their masters, for any slavery or tyranny is easier than love's. – Come hither. Since thou art so forward to serve me, hast thou but resolution enough to endure the torture of a secret? For such to some is insupportable.

FIDELIA.
I would keep it as safe as if your dear precious life depended on't.

MANLY.
Damn your dearness. It concerns more than my life, my honour.

FIDELIA.
Doubt it not, sir.

MANLY.
[And do not discover it by too much fear of discovering it,] but have a great care you let not Freeman find it out.

FIDELIA.
I warrant you, sir. I am already all joy with the hopes of your commands [and shall be all wings in the execution of 'em.] Speak quickly, sir.

MANLY.
You said you would beg for me.

FIDELIA.
I did, sir.

MANLY.
Then you shall beg for me.

FIDELIA.
With all my heart, sir.

MANLY.
That is, pimp for me.

FIDELIA.
How, sir?

MANLY.
D'ye start! Thinkst thou, thou couldst do me any other service? Come, no dissembling honour. I know you can do it handsomely; thou wert made for't. You have lost your time with me at sea; you must recover it.

FIDELIA.
Do not, sir, beget yourself more reasons for your aversion to me and make my obedience to you a fault. I am the unfittest in the world to do you such a service.

MANLY.
Your cunning arguing against it shows but how fit you are for it. No more dissembling. Here, I say, you must go use it for me to Olivia.

FIDELIA.
To her, sir?

MANLY.
Go flatter, lie, kneel, promise, anything to get her for me. I cannot live unless I have her. Didst thou not say thou wouldst do anything to save my life? And she said you had a persuading face.

FIDELIA.
But did not you say, sir, your honour was dearer to you than your life? And would you have me contribute to the loss of that and carry love from you to the most infamous, most false and –

MANLY.
And most beautiful! (*Sighs aside.*)

FIDELIA.
Most ungrateful woman that ever lived, for sure she must be so that could [desert you so soon,] use you so basely, [and so lately too.] Do not, do not forget it, sir, and think –

MANLY.
No, I will not forget it but think of revenge. I will lie with her, out of revenge. Go, be gone, and prevail for me or never see me more.

FIDELIA.
You scorned her last night.

MANLY.
I know not what I did last night. I dissembled last night.

FIDELIA.
Heavens!

MANLY.
Be gone, I say, and bring me love or compliance back, o hopes at least, or I'll never see thy face again. By –

FIDELIA.
O do not swear, sir. First hear me.

MANLY.
I am impatient. Away. You'll find me here till twelve. (*Turn away.*)

FIDELIA.
Sir –

MANLY.
Not one word, [no insinuating argument more or soothin persuasion; you'll have need of all your rhetoric with her.] Go strive to alter her, not me. Be gone.

Exit Manly at the end of the stag

FIDELIA.
Should I discover to him now my sex
And lay before him his strange cruelty,
'Twould but incense it more. – No, 'tis not time.
For his love, must I then betray my own?
Were ever love or chance, till now, severe?
Or shifting woman posed with such a task?
Forced to beg that which kills her if obtained
And give away her lover not to lose him.

Exit Fideli

Enter Widow Blackacre in the middle of half a dozen lawyer. whispered to by a fellow in black, Jerry Blackacre following th crowd.

[WIDOW.
Offer me a reference, you saucy companion you! D'ye kno who you speak to? Art thou a solicitor in Chancery and offer reference? A pretty fellow! Mr Serjeant Ploddon, here's fellow has the impudence to offer me a reference.

SERJEANT PLODDON.
Who's that has the impudence to offer a reference withi these walls?

WIDOW.
Nay, for a splitter of causes to do't!

SERJEANT PLODDON.
No, madam, to a lady learned in the law as you are the offer of a reference were to impose upon you.

WIDOW.
No, no, never fear me for a reference, Mr Serjeant. But, come, have you not forgot your brief? Are you sure you shan't make the mistake of – hark you – (*Whispers.*) Go then, go to your Court of Common Pleas and say one thing over and over again. You do it so naturally, you'll never be suspected for protracting time.

SERJEANT PLODDON.
Come, I know the course of the court, and your business.

Exit Serjeant Ploddon.]

WIDOW.
Let's see, Jerry, where are my minutes? Come, Mr Quaint, pray, go talk a great deal for me in Chancery. Let your words be easy and your sense hard; my cause requires it. Branch it bravely and deck my cause with flowers that the snake may lie hidden. [Go, go, and be sure you remember the decree of my Lord Chancellor *tricesimo quart'* of the Queen.

QUAINT.
I will, as I see cause, extenuate or examplify matter of fact, baffle truth with impudence, answer exceptions with questions, though never so impertinent, for reasons give 'em words, for law and equity, tropes and figures; and so relax and enervate the sinews of their argument with the oil of my eloquence. But when my lungs can reason no longer, and not being able to say anything more for our cause, say everything of our adversary, whose reputation, though never so clear and evident in the eye of the world, yet with sharp invectives –

WIDOW (*aside*).
Alias Billingsgate.

QUAINT.
With poignant and sour invectives, I say, I will deface, wipe out and obliterate his fair reputation, even as a record with the juice of lemons, and tell such a story – for the truth on't is, all that we can do for our client in Chancery is telling a story – a fine story, a long story, such a story –

WIDOW.
Go, save thy breath for the cause; talk at the bar, Mr Quaint. You are so copiously fluent you can weary anyone's ears sooner than your own tongue. Go, weary our adversary's counsel and the court. Go, thou art a fine-spoken person.

Adad, I shall make thy wife jealous of me if you can but court the court into a decree for us.] Go, get you gone, and remember – (*Whispers.*)

Exit Quaint.

[Come, Mr Blunder, pray bawl soundly for me at the King's Bench, bluster, sputter, question, cavil, but be sure your argument be intricate enough to confound the court, and then you do my business. Talk what you will but be sure your tongue never stand still, for your own noise will secure your sense from censure – 'tis like coughing or hemming when one has got the bellyache, which stifles the unmannerly noise. Go, dear rogue, and succeed and I'll invite thee, ere it be long, to more soused venison.

BLUNDER.
I'll warrant you, after your verdict your judgement shall not be arrested upon ifs and ands.

Exit Blunder]

¹

WIDOW.
Come, Mr Petulant, let me give you some new instructions for our cause in the Exchequer. Are the barons sat?

PETULANT.
Yes, no. May be they are, may be they are not. What know I? What care I?

WIDOW.
Hey-day! I wish you would [but snap up the counsel on t'other side anon, at the bar, as much and] have a little more patience with me that I might instruct you a little better.

PETULANT.
You instruct me! What is my brief for, mistress?

WIDOW.
Ay, but you seldom read your brief but at the bar, if you do it then.

PETULANT.
Perhaps I do, perhaps I don't, [and perhaps 'tis time enough.] Pray hold yourself contented, mistress.

WIDOW.
Nay, [if you go there too, I will not be contented, sir. Though you, I see, will lose my cause for want of speaking, I won't.] You shall hear me and shall be instructed. Let's see your brief.

---

¹*Insert:* dialogue given between braces from p.36.

PETULANT.

Send your solicitor to me. Instructed by a woman! [I'd have you to know, I do not wear a bar-gown –]

WIDOW.

By a woman! And I'd have you to know, I am no common woman but a woman conversant in the laws of the land, as well as yourself, though I have no bar-gown.

PETULANT.

Go to, go to, mistress. You are impertinent, and there's your brief for you. Instruct me! (*Flings her breviate at her.*)

WIDOW.

Impertinent to me, you saucy Jack you! You return my breviate but where's my fee? [You'll be sure to keep that and scan that so well that if there chance to be but a brass half-crown in't, one's sure to hear on't again. Would you would but look on your breviate half so narrowly. But] pray give me my fee too as well as my brief.

PETULANT.

Mistress, that's without precedent. When did a counsel ever return his fee, pray? And you are impertinent, and ignorant, to demand it.

WIDOW.

Impertinent again and ignorant to me! Gadsbodikins, you puny upstart in the law, to use me so, you green bag carrier, you murderer of unfortunate causes. The clerk's ink is scarce off of your fingers, you that newly come from lamp-blacking the judge's shoes and are not fit to wipe mine. You call me impertinent and ignorant! I would give thee a cuff on the ear, sitting the courts, if I were ignorant. Marry gep, if it had not been for me, thou hadst been yet but a hearing counsel at the bar.

Exit Petulant.

{ [*Enter Mr Buttongown[2] crossing the stage in haste.*]

Mr Buttongown,[2] Mr Buttongown,[2] whither so fast? What, won't you stay till we are heard?

BUTTONGOWN[2]

I cannot, Mrs Blackacre, I must be at the Council; my lord's cause stays there for me.

WIDOW.

And mine suffers here.

[2]. PETULANT

BUTTONGOWN[2]

I cannot help it.

WIDOW.

I'm undone.

BUTTONGOWN[2]

What's that to me?

WIDOW.

Consider the five pound fee if not my cause – that was something to you.

BUTTONGOWN[2]

Away, away, pray be not so troublesome, mistress. I must be gone.

[WIDOW.

Nay, but consider a little. I am your old client, my lord but a new one; or, let him be what he will, he will hardly be a better client to you than myself. I hope you believe I shall be in law as long as I live, therefore am no despicable client. Well, but go to your lord. I know you expect he should make you a judge one day; but I hope this promise to you will prove a true lord's promise. But that he might be sure to fail you I wish you had his bond for't.

BUTTONGOWN[2]

But, what, will you yet be thus impertinent, mistress?

WIDOW.

Nay I beseech you, sir, stay, if it be but to tell me my lord's case. Come, in short.]

BUTTONGOWN[2]

Nay then –

Exit Buttongown.[2] }

WIDOW.

Well, Jerry, observe, child, and lay it up for hereafter: these are those lawyers who by being in all causes are in none; therefore if you would have 'em for you, let your adversary fee 'em, for he may chance to depend upon 'em, and so in being against thee they'll be for thee.

JERRY.

Ay, mother, they put me in mind of the unconscionable wooers of widows, who undertake briskly their matrimonial business for their money, but when they have got it once, let who's will drudge for them; therefore have a care of 'em, forsooth. There's advice for your advice.

WIDOW.

Well said, boy. Come, Mr Splitcause, pray go see when my cause in Chancery comes on; and go speak with Mr Quillet in the King's Bench and Mr Quirk in the Common Pleas and see how our matters go there.

Enter Major Oldfox.

OLDFOX.

Lady, a good and propitious morning to you, and may all your causes go as well as if I myself were judge of 'em.

WIDOW.

Sir, excuse me, I am busy and cannot answer compliments in Westminster Hall. Go, Mr Splitcause, and come to me again to that bookseller's – there I'll stay for you that you may be sure to find me.

OLDFOX.

No, sir, come to the other bookseller's, [I'll attend your lady-ship thither.]

Exit Splitcause

WIDOW.

Why to the other?

OLDFOX.

Because he is my bookseller, lady.

WIDOW.

What, to sell you lozenges for your catarrh? Or medicines for your corns? What else can a major deal with a bookseller for?

OLDFOX.

Lady, he prints for me.

WIDOW.

Why, are you an author?

OLDFOX.

Of some few essays. Deign you, lady, to peruse 'em (*Aside.*) She is a woman of parts and I must win her by showing mine.

BOOKSELLER'S BOY.

Will you see [Culpepper, mistress? Aristotle's 'Problems'?] 'The Compleat Midwife'?

WIDOW.

No, let's see Dalton, Hughes, Shepherd, Wingate.

BOY.

We have no lawbooks.

WIDOW.

No? You are a pretty bookseller then.

OLDFOX.

Come, have you e'er a one of my essays left?

BOY.

Yes, sir, we have enough, and shall always have 'em.

OLDFOX.

How so?

BOY.

Why, they are good, steady, lasting ware.

OLDFOX.

Nay, I hope they will live. Let's see. Be pleased, madam, to peruse the poor endeavours of my pen, for I have a pen, though I say it, that – (*Gives her a book.*)

JERRY.

Pray let me see 'St George for Christendom' or 'The Seven Champions of England.'

WIDOW.

No, no, give him 'The Young Clerk's Guide'. What, we shall have you read yourself into a humour of rambling and fighting and studying military discipline and wearing red breeches!

OLDFOX.

Nay, if you talk of military discipline, show him my treatise of 'The Art Military'.

WIDOW.

Hold, I would as willingly he should read a play.

JERRY.

O pray, forsooth, mother, let me have a play.

WIDOW.

No, sirrah, there are young students of the law enough spoiled already by plays; they would make you in love with your laundress or, what's worse, some queen of the stage that was a laundress, [and so turn keeper before you are of age.]

Several crossing the stage.

But stay, Jerry, is not that Mr What-d'y'call-him that goes there, he that offered to sell me a suit in Chancery for five hundred pound, for a hundred down and only paying the clerks' fees?

JERRY.

Ay, forsooth, 'tis he.

WIDOW.

Then stay here and have a care of the bags whilst I follow him. Have a care of the bags, I say.

JERRY.

And do you have a care, forsooth, of the statute against champerty, I say.

Exit Widow.

Enter Freeman.

FREEMAN (*aside*).

So, there's a limb of my widow which was wont to be inseparable from her. She can't be far. – How now, my pretty son-in-law that shall be, where's my widow?

JERRY.

My mother, but not your widow, will be forthcoming presently.

FREEMAN.

Your servant, major. What, are you buying furniture for a little sleeping closet which you miscall a study? For you do only by your books as by your wenches, bind 'em up neatly and make 'em fine, for other people to use 'em; and your bookseller is properly your upholster, for he furnishes your room rather than your head.

OLDFOX.

[Well, well,] good sea-lieutenant, study you your compass that's more than your head can deal with. (*Aside.*) I will go find out the widow to keep her out of his sight, or he'll board her whilst I am treating a peace.

Exit Oldfox.

JERRY.

Nay, prithee, friend, now let me have but the 'Seven Champions'. You shall trust me no longer than till my mother's Mr Splitcause comes, for I hope he'll lend me wherewithal to pay for't.

FREEMAN.

Lend thee! Here, I'll pay him. Do you want money, squire? I'm sorry a man of your estate should want money.

JERRY.

Nay, my mother will ne'er let me be at age. And till then she says –

FREEMAN.

At age! Why, you are at age already to have spent an estate, man; there are younger than you have kept their women these three years, have had half a dozen claps, and lost as many thousand pounds at play.

JERRY.

Ay, they are happy sparks! Nay, I know some of my school-fellows who when we were at school were two years younger than me but now, I know not how, are grown men before me and go where they will and look to themselves, but my curmudgeonly mother won't allow me wherewithal to be a man of myself with.

FREEMAN.

Why, there 'tis. I knew your mother was in the fault. Ask but your schoolfellows what they did to be men of themselves.

JERRY.

Why, I know they went to law with their mothers, for they say there's no good to be done upon a widow-mother till one goes to law with her, but mine is as plaguey a lawyer as any's of our Inn. Then would she marry too and cut down my trees. Now I should hate, man, to have my father's wife kissed and slapped and t'other thing too (you know what I mean) by another man, and our trees are the purest, tall, even, shady twigs, by my fa –

FREEMAN.

Come, squire, let your mother and your trees fall as she pleases rather than wear this gown and carry green bags all thy life and be pointed at for a tony. But you shall be able to deal with her yet the common way; thou shalt make false love to some lawyer's daughter, whose father, upon the hopes of thy marrying her, shall lend the money, and law, to preserve thy estate and trees, and thy mother is so ugly nobody will have her if she cannot cut down thy trees.

JERRY.

Nay, if I had but anybody to stand by me, I am as stomachful as another.

FREEMAN.

That will I. I'll not see any hopeful young gentleman abused.

BOY (*aside*).

By any but yourself.

JERRY.

The truth on't is, mine's as arrant a widow-mother to her poor child as any's in England: she won't so much as let one have sixpence in one's pocket to see a motion or the dancing of the ropes or –

FREEMAN.

Come, you shan't want money. There's gold for you.

JERRY.

O Lurd, sir, two guineas! D'ye lend me this? Is there no trick in't? Well, sir, I'll give you my bond for security.

FREEMAN.

No, no, thou hast given me thy face for security. Anybody would swear thou dost not look like a cheat. You shall have what you will of me and, if your mother will not be kinder to you, come to me, who will.

JERRY (aside).

By my fa – he's a curious fine gentleman! – But, will you stand by one?

FREEMAN.

If you can be resolute.

JERRY.

Can be resolved! Gad, if she gives me but a cross word, I'll leave her tonight and come to you. But now I have got money I'll go to Jack of All Trades, at t'other end of the Hall, and buy the neatest, purest things –

FREEMAN (aside).

And I'll follow the great boy and my blow at his mother. Steal away the calf and the cow will follow you.

Exit Jerry, followed by Freeman.

Enter, on the other side, Manly, Widow Blackacre and Oldfox.

MANLY.

Damn your cause; can't you lose it without me? [Which you are like enough to do if it be, as you say, an honest one.] I will suffer no longer for't.

WIDOW.

Nay, captain, I tell you, you are my prime witness and the cause is just now coming on, Mr Splitcause tells me. Lord, methinks you should take a pleasure in walking here as half you see now do, for they have no business here, I assure you.

MANLY.

Yes, but I'll assure you then, their business is to persecute me. [But d'ye think I'll stay any longer, to have a rogue, because he knows my name, pluck me aside and whisper a newsbook-secret to me with a stinking breath? A second come piping angry from the court and sputter in my face his tedious complaints against it? A third law-coxcomb, because he saw me once at a Reader's dinner, come and put me a long law-case, to make discovery of his indefatigable dullness and my wearied patience? A fourth, a most barbarous civil rogue, who will keep a man half an hour in the crowd with a bowed body and a hat off, acting the reformed sign of the Salutation Tavern, to hear his bountiful professions of service and friendship, whilst he cares not if I were damned and I am wishing him hanged out of my way?] I'd as soon run the gauntlet as walk t'other turn.

Enter Jerry Blackacre without his bags but laden with trinkets, which he endeavours to hide from his mother, and followed at a distance by Freeman.

WIDOW.

O, are you come, sir? But where have you been, you ass? And how come you thus laden?

JERRY.

Look here, forsooth mother, now here's a duck, here's a boar-cat and here's an owl. (*Making a noise with catcalls and other suchlike instruments.*)

WIDOW.

Yes, there is an owl, sir.

OLDFOX.

He's an ungracious bird, indeed.

WIDOW.

But go, thou trangame, and carry back those trangames which thou hast stolen or purloined, for nobody would trust a minor in Westminster Hall, sure.

JERRY.

Hold yourself contented, forsooth. I have these commodities by a fair bargain and sale, and there stands my witness and creditor.

WIDOW.

How's that! What, sir, d'ye think to get the mother by giving the child a rattle? But where are my bags, my writings, you rascal?

JERRY (aside).

O law! Where are they indeed?

WIDOW.

How, sirrah? Speak, come –

MANLY (*apart to him*).

You can tell her, Freeman, I suppose?

FREEMAN (*apart to him*).

'Tis true, I made one of your salt-water sharks steal 'em,

whilst he was eagerly choosing his commodities, as he calls 'em, [in order to my design upon his mother.]

WIDOW.
Won't you speak? Where were you, I say, you son of a – an unfortunate woman? O major, I'm undone. They are all that concern my estate, my jointure, my husband's deed of gift, my evidences for all my suits now depending! What will become of them?

FREEMAN (*aside*).
I'm glad to hear this. – They'll be safe, I warrant you madam.

WIDOW.
O where? Where? Come, you villain, along with me and show me where.

Exeunt Widow, Jerry, Oldfox.

MANLY.
[Thou hast taken the right way to get a widow, by making her great boy revel, for when nothing will make a widow marry she'll do't to cross her children. But] canst thou in earnest marry this harpy, this volume of shrivelled, blurred parchments and law, [this attorney's desk?]

FREEMAN.
Ay, ay, I'll marry and live honestly, that is, give my creditors, not her, due benevolence, pay my debts.

MANLY.
Thy creditors, you see, are not so barbarous as to put thee in prison; and wilt thou commit thyself to a noisome dungeon for thy life, which is the only satisfaction thou canst give thy creditors by this match?

FREEMAN.
Why, is not she rich?

MANLY.
Ay, but he that marries a widow for her money will find himself as much mistaken as the widow that marries a young fellow for due benevolence, as you call it.

FREEMAN.
Why, d'ye think I shan't deserve wages? I'll drudge faithfully.

MANLY.
I tell thee again, he that is the slave in the mine has the least propriety in the core. You may dig and dig, but if thou wouldst have her money rather get to be her trustee than her husband, for a true widow will make over her estate to anybody and cheat herself rather than be cheated by her children or a second husband.

Enter Jerry, running in a fright.

JERRY.
O law! I'm undone, I'm undone, My mother will kill me. You said you'd stand by one.

FREEMAN.
So I will, my brave squire, I warrant thee.

JERRY.
Ay, but I dare not stay till she comes, for she's as furious, now she has lost her writings, as a bitch when she has lost her puppies.

MANLY.
The comparison's handsome!

JERRY.
O, she's here!

Enter Widow Blackacre and Oldfox.

FREEMAN (*to the Sailor*).
Take him, Jack, and make haste with him to your [master's] lodging; and be sure you keep him up till I come.

Exeunt Jerry and Sailor.

WIDOW.
O my dear writings! Where's this heathen rogue, my minor?

FREEMAN.
Gone to drown or hang himself.

WIDOW.
No, I know him too well, he'll ne'er be *felo de se* that way; but he may go and choose a guardian of his own head and so be *felo de ses biens*: for he has not yet chosen one.

FREEMAN (*aside*).
Say you so? And he shan't want one.

WIDOW.
But, now I think on't, 'tis you, sir, have put this cheat upon me; for there is a saying, 'Take hold of a maid by her smock and a widow by her writings and they cannot get from you. But I'll play fast and loose with you yet, if there be law; and my minor and writings are not forthcoming, I'll bring my action of detinue or trover. But first I'll try to find out this guardianless, graceless villain. Will you jog, major?

MANLY.

If you have lost your evidence, I hope your causes cannot go on and I may be gone?

WIDOW.

O no, stay but a making-water while, as one may say, and I'll be with you again.

Exeunt Widow and Oldfox.

FREEMAN.

Well, sure I am the first man that ever began a love intrigue in Westminster Hall.

MANLY.

No, sure, for the love to a widow generally begins here. [And as the widow's cause goes against the heir or executors, the jointure rivals commence their suit to the widow.]

FREEMAN

[Well,] but how, pray, have you passed your time here since I was forced to leave you alone? You have had a great deal of patience.

MANLY.

Is this a place to be alone or have patience in? But I have had patience indeed, for I have drawn upon me, since I came, but three quarrels and two lawsuits.

FREEMAN.

Nay, faith, you are too cursed to be let loose in the world; you should be tied up again in your sea-kennel called a ship. But how could you quarrel here?

MANLY.

How could I refrain? A lawyer talked peremptorily and saucily to me and as good as gave me the lie.

FREEMAN.

They do it so often to one another at the bar that they make no bones on't elsewhere.

MANLY.

However, I gave him a cuff on the ear; whereupon he jogs two men, whose backs were turned to us, for they were reading at a bookseller's, to witness I struck him, [sitting the courts,] which office they so readily promised that I called 'em rascals and knights of the post. One of 'em presently calls two other absent witnesses [who were coming towards us at a distance,] whilst the other with a whisper desires to know my name that he might have satisfaction by way of challenge as t'other by way of writ; [but if it were not rather to direct his brother's

writ than his own challenge.] There you see is one of my quarrels and two of my lawsuits.

FREEMAN.

So – and the other two?

MANLY.

For advising a poet to leave off writing and turn lawyer because he is dull and impudent [and says or writes nothing now but by precedent.]

FREEMAN.

And the third quarrel?

MANLY.

For giving more sincere advice to a handsome, well-dressed young fellow (who asked it too) not to marry a wench that he loved and I had lain with.

FREEMAN.

Nay, if you will be giving your sincere advice to lovers and poets you will not fail of quarrels.

MANLY.

Or if I stay in this place, for I see more quarrels crowding upon me. Let's be gone and avoid 'em.

Enter Novel, at a distance, coming towards them.

A plague on him, that sneer is ominous to us; [he is coming upon us and we shall not be rid of him.]

NOVEL.

Dear bully, don't look so grum upon me; you told me just now you had forgiven me a little harmless raillery upon wooden legs last night.

MANLY.

Yes, yes, pray be gone. I am talking of business.

NOVEL.

Can't I hear it? I love thee and will be faithful and always –

MANLY.

Impertinent! 'Tis business that concerns Freeman only.

NOVEL.

Well, I love Freeman too and would not divulge his secret. Prithee speak, prithee, [I must –]

MANLY.

[Prithee, let me be rid of thee.] I must be rid of thee.

NOVEL.

Faith, [thou canst hardly,] I love thee so. Come, I must know the business.

MANLY (*aside*).

[So, I have it now.] – Why, if you needs will know it, he has a quarrel and his adversary bids him bring two friends with him. Now, I am one and we are thinking who we shall have for a third.

Several crossing the stage.

NOVEL.

A pox, there goes a fellow owes me an hundred pound and goes out of town tomorrow. I'll speak with him and come to you presently.

Exit Novel.

MANLY.

No but you won't.

FREEMAN.

You are dextrously rid of him.

Enter Oldfox.

MANLY.

To what purpose, since here comes another as impertinent? I know by his grin he is bound hither.

OLDFOX.

Your servant, worthy, noble captain. Well, I have left the widow because she carried me from your company, for, faith, captain, I must needs tell thee thou art the only officer in England who was not an Edgehill officer that I care for.

MANLY.

I'm sorry for't.

OLDFOX.

Why, wouldst thou have me love them!

MANLY.

Anybody rather than me.

OLDFOX.

What, you are modest, I see! Therefore too I love thee.

MANLY.

No, I am not modest but love to brag myself and can't patiently hear you fight over the last civil war; [therefore go look out the fellow I saw just now here, that walks with his stockings and his sword out at heels, and let him tell you the history of that scar on his cheek, to give you occasion to show yours, got in the field at Bloomsbury, not that of Edgehill. Go to him, poor fellow. He is fasting and has not yet the happi-

ness this morning to stink of brandy and tobacco; go, give him some to hear you.] I am busy.

OLDFOX.

Well, ygad, I love thee now, boy, for thy surliness. Thou ar no tame captain, I see, that will suffer –

[MANLY.

An old fox.]

OLDFOX.

[All] that shan't make me angry. I consider thou art peevish and fretting at some ill success at law. Prithee tell me what il luck you have met with here.

MANLY.

You.

OLDFOX

Do I look like the picture of ill luck? Gadsnouns, I love the more and more; and shall I tell thee what made me love the first?

[MANLY.

Do, that I may be rid of that damned quality and thee.]

OLDFOX.

'Twas thy wearing that broad sword there.

MANLY.

Here, Freeman, let's change. I'll never wear it more.

OLDFOX.

How! You won't sure. Prithee don't look like one of ou holiday captains nowadays, with a bodkin by your side, you Martinet rogues.

MANLY (*aside*).

[O, then there's hopes. –] What, d'ye find faults with Martinet? Let me tell you, sir, 'tis the best exercise in the world, the most ready, most easy, most graceful exercise tha ever was used and the most –

OLDFOX.

Nay, nay, sir, no more, sir, your servant. If you prais [Martinet] once, I have done with you, sir. [Martinet Martinet!]

Exit Oldfox

FREEMAN.

Nay, you had made him leave you as willingly as ever he di an enemy, for he was truly for the king and parliament: fo the parliament in their list and for the king in cheating 'em o their pay and never hurting the king's party in the field.

Enter a Lawyer towards them.

MANLY.

A pox! This way; here's a lawyer I know threatening us with another greeting.

LAWYER.

Sir, sir, your very servant. I was afraid you had forgotten me.

MANLY.

I was not afraid you had forgotten me.

[LAWYER.

No, sir, we lawyers have pretty good memories.

MANLY.

You ought to have, by your wits.]

LAWYER.

O, you are a merry gentleman, sir. [I remember you were merry when I was last in your company.

MANLY.

I was never merry in your company, Mr Lawyer, sure.

LAWYER.

Why, I'm sure you joked upon me and shammed me all night long.

MANLY.

Shammed! Prithee, what barbarous law-term is that?

LAWYER.

Shamming! Why, don't you know that? 'Tis all our way of wit, sir.

MANLY.

I am glad I do not know it then. Shamming! What does he mean by't, Freeman?

FREEMAN.

Shamming is telling you an insipid, dull lie, with a dull face, which the sly wag the author only laughs at himself, and making himself believe 'tis a good jest, puts the sham only upon himself.

MANLY.

So, your lawyer's jest, I find, like his practice, has more knavery than wit in't. I should make the worst shammer in England. I must always deal ingeniously, as I will with you, Mr Lawyer, and advise you to be seen rather with attornies

and solicitors then such fellows as I am; they will credit your practice more.

LAWYER.

No, sir, your company's an honour to me.

MANLY.

No, faith, go this way, there goes an attorney; leave me for him. Let it be never said a lawyer's civility did him hurt.

LAWYER.

No, worthy, honoured sir, I'll not leave you for any attorney, sure.

MANLY.

Unless he had a fee in his hand.]

LAWYER.

Have you any business here, sir? Try me. [I'd serve you sooner than any attorney breathing.]

MANLY.

Business! (*Aside.*) [So, I have thought of a sure way.] – Yes, faith, I have a little business.

LAWYER.

Have you so, sir? [In what court, sir?] What is't, sir? Tell me but how I may serve you and I'll do't, sir, and take it for as great an honour –

MANLY.

Faith, 'tis for a poor orphan of a sea-officer of mine that has no money; but if it could be followed *in forma pauperis*, [and when the legacy's recovered –]

LAWYER.

Forma pauperis, sir!

MANLY.

Ay, sir.

Several crossing the stage.

LAWYER.

Mr Bumblecase, Mr Bumblecase, a word with you. – Sir, I beg your pardon at present, I have a little business –

MANLY.

Which is not *in forma pauperis*.

Exit Lawyer.

FREEMAN.

So, you have now found a way to be rid of people without quarrelling.

Enter Alderman.

MANLY.

But here's a city rogue will stick as hard upon us as if I owed him money.

ALDERMAN.

Captain, noble sir, I am yours heartily, d'ye see. Why should you avoid your old friends?

MANLY.

And why should you follow me? I owe you nothing.

[ALDERMAN.

Out of my hearty respects to you, for there is not a man in England –

MANLY.

Thou wouldst save from hanging with the expense of a shilling only.

ALDERMAN.

Nay, nay, but captain, you are like enough to tell me –

MANLY.

Truth, which you won't care to hear; therefore you had better go talk with somebody else.]

ALDERMAN.

[No,] I know nobody can inform me better of some young wit or spendthrift that has a good dipped seat and estate in Middlesex, Hertfordshire, Essex or Kent – any of these would serve my turn. Now, if you knew of such an one and would but help –

MANLY.

You to finish his ruin.

ALDERMAN.

I'faith, you should have a snip –

MANLY.

Of your nose. You thirty in the hundred rascal, would you make me your squire setter, your bawd for manors? (*Takes him by the nose.*)

ALDERMAN.

Oh!

FREEMAN.

Hold or here will be your third lawsuit.

ALDERMAN.

Gad's precious, you hectoring person you, are you wild? I meant you no hurt, sir. I begin to think, as things go, land

security best and have, for a convenient mortgage, some ten, fifteen or twenty thousand pound by me.

MANLY.

Then go lay it out upon an hospital [and take a mortgage of heaven according to your city custom, for you think by laying out a little money to hook in that too hereafter. Do, I say, and] keep the poor you've made by taking forfeitures [that heaven may not take yours.]

ALDERMAN.

No, to keep the cripples you make this war; this war spoils our trade.

MANLY.

Damn your trade; 'tis the better for't.

ALDERMAN.

What, will you speak against our trade?

MANLY.

And dare you speak against the war, our trade?

ALDERMAN (*aside*).

Well, he may be a convoy of ships I am concerned in. – [Come, captain, I will have a fair correspondency with you say what you will.]

[MANLY.

Then prithee be gone.]

ALDERMAN.

No, faith, prithee, captain, let's go drink a dish of laced coffee and talk of the times. Come, I'll treat you. Nay, you shall go for I have no business here.

MANLY.

But I have.

ALDERMAN.

To pick up a man to give thee a dinner? Come, I'll do thy business for thee.

MANLY.

Faith, now I think on't, so you may, as well as any man, for 'tis to pick up a man to be bound with me to one who expect city security, [for –]

ALDERMAN.

Nay, then your servant, captain. Business must be done.

MANLY.

Ay, if it can, but hark you, alderman, without you –

ALDERMAN.

Business, sir, I say, must be done, and there's an officer of the Treasury I have an affair with –

Several crossing the stage.

Exit Alderman.

MANLY.

You see now what the mighty friendship of the world is, [what all ceremony, embraces and plentiful professions come to. You are no more to believe a professing friend than a threatening enemy and, as no man hurts you that tells you he'll do you a mischief, no man, you see, is your servant who says he is so.] Why the devil, then, should a man be troubled with the flattery of knaves, if he be not a fool or cully, or with the fondness of fools, if he be not a knave or cheat?

FREEMAN.

Only for his pleasure, for there is some in laughing at fools and disappointing knaves.

MANLY.

That's a pleasure, I think, would cost you too dear, as well as marrying your widow to disappoint her; but, for my part, I have no pleasure by 'em, but in despising 'em, wheresoe'er I meet 'em, [and then the pleasure of hoping so to be rid of 'em.] But now my comfort is, I am not worth a shilling in the world, which all the world shall know; and then I'm sure I shall have none of 'em come near me.

FREEMAN.

A very pretty comfort, which I think you pay too dear for. But is the twenty pound gone since the morning?

MANLY.

To my boat's crew. Would you have the poor, honest, brave fellows want?

FREEMAN.

Rather than you or I.

MANLY.

Why, art thou without money? Thou who art a friend to everybody?

FREEMAN.

I ventured my last stake upon the squire, to nick him of his mother and cannot help you to a dinner, unless you will go dine with my lord –

MANLY.

No, no, the ordinary is too dear for me, where flattery must pay for my dinner; I am no [herald, or] poet.

FREEMAN.

We'll go then to the bishop's –

MANLY.

There you must flatter the old philosophy. I cannot renounce my reason for a dinner.

FREEMAN.

Why, then let's go to your alderman's.

MANLY.

Hang him, rogue! That were not to dine, for he makes you drunk with lees of sack before dinner to take away your stomach and there you must call usury and extortion, God's blessings or the honest turning of the penny; [hear him brag of the leather breeches in which he trotted first to town, and make a greater noise with his money in his parlour than his cashiers do in his counting-house, without hopes of borrowing a shilling.]

FREEMAN.

Ay, a pox on't, ['tis like dining with the great gamesters and, when they fall to their common dessert, see the heaps of gold drawn on all hands, without going to twelve.] Let us go to my Lady Goodly's.

MANLY.

There to flatter her looks you must mistake her grandchildren for her own, [praise her cook that she may rail at him and feed her dogs, not yourself.]

FREEMAN.

What d'ye think of eating with your lawyer then?

MANLY.

Eat with him! [Damn him, to hear him employ his barbarous eloquence in a reading upon the two and thirty good bits in a shoulder of veal and be forced yourself to praise the cold bribe pie that stinks and drink law-French wine as rough and harsh as his law-French.] A pox on him, I'd rather dine [in the Temple Rounds or Walks,] with [the knights without noses, or] the knights of the post, who are honester fellows and better company. But let us home and try our fortune, for I'll stay no longer here for your damned widow.

FREEMAN.

Well, let us go home then, for I must go for my damned widow and look after my new damned charge. Three or four hundred years ago a man might have dined in this hall.

MANLY.

But now, the lawyer only here is fed
And, bullylike, by quarrels gets his bread.

Exeunt.

ACT FOUR

Scene One

Manly's lodging. Enter Manly and Fidelia.

MANLY.
Well, there's success in thy face. Hast thou prevailed? Say.

FIDELIA.
As I could wish, sir.

MANLY.
So, I told thee what thou wert fit for and thou wouldst not believe me. Come, thank me for bringing thee acquainted with thy genius. Well, thou hast mollified her heart for me?

FIDELIA.
No, sir, not so, but what's better.

MANLY.
How? What's better!

FIDELIA.
I shall harden your heart against her.

MANLY.
Have a care, sir. My heart is too much in earnest to be fooled with and my desire at heighth and needs no delays to incite it. What, you are too good a pimp already and know how to endear pleasure by withholding it? But leave off your page's bawdyhouse tricks, sir, and tell me; will she be kind?

FIDELIA.
Kinder than you could wish, sir.

MANLY.
So then. Well, prithee what said she?

FIDELIA.
She said –

MANLY.
What? Thou'rt so tedious. Speak comfort to me. What?

FIDELIA.
That, of all things, you were her aversion.

MANLY.
How?

FIDELIA.
That she would sooner take a bedfellow out of an hospital and diseases into her arms than you.

MANLY.
What?

FIDELIA.
That she would rather trust her honour with a dissolute, debauched hector, nay worse, with a finical, baffled coward, all over loathsome with affectation of the fine gentleman.

MANLY.
What's all this you say?

FIDELIA.
Nay, that my offers of your love to her were more offensive than when parents woo their virgin daughters to the enjoyment of riches only and that you were in all circumstances as nauseous to her as a husband on compulsion.

MANLY.
Hold, I understand you not.

FIDELIA (*aside*).
So, 'twill work, I see.

MANLY.
Did not you tell me –

FIDELIA.
She called you ten thousand ruffians.

MANLY.
Hold, I say,

FIDELIA.
Brutes –

MANLY.
Hold.

FIDELIA.
Sea-monsters –

MANLY.
Damn your intelligence. Hear me a little now.

FIDELIA.
Nay, surly coward she called you too.

MANLY.
Won't you hold yet? Hold, or –

FIDELIA.
Nay, sir, pardon me. I could not but tell you she had the baseness, the injustice, to call you coward, sir, coward, coward, sir.

MANLY.

Not yet?

FIDELIA.

I've done. Coward, sir.

MANLY.

Did not you say she was kinder than I could wish her?

FIDELIA.

Yes sir.

MANLY.

How then? – O – I understand you now. At first she appeared in rage and disdain, the truest sign of a coming woman, but at last you prevailed, it seems; did you not?

FIDELIA.

Yes, sir.

MANLY.

So then, let's know that only. Come, prithee, without delays. I'll kiss thee for that news beforehand.

FIDELIA (aside).

So, the kiss, I'm sure, is welcome to me, whatsoe'er the news will be to you.

MANLY.

Come, speak, my dear volunteer.

FIDELIA (aside).

How welcome were that kind word too, if it were not for another woman's sake!

MANLY.

What, won't you speak? You prevailed for me at last, you say?

FIDELIA.

No, sir.

MANLY.

No more of your fooling, sir; it will not agree with my impatience or temper.

FIDELIA.

Then, not to fool you, sir, I spoke to her for you but prevailed for myself. She would not hear me when I spoke in your behalf but bid me say what I would in my own – though she gave me no occasion, she was so coming – and so was kinder, sir, than you could wish, which I was only afraid to let you know without some warning.

MANLY.

How's this? Young man, you are of a lying age, but I must hear you out, and if –

FIDELIA.

I would not abuse you and cannot wrong her by any report of her, she is so wicked.

MANLY.

How, wicked! Had she the impudence, at the second sight of you only –

FIDELIA.

Impudence, sir! O, she has impudence enough to put a court out of countenance and debauch a stews.

MANLY.

Why, what said she?

FIDELIA.

Her tongue, I confess, was silent, but her speaking eyes gloated such things, more immodest and lascivious than ravishers can act or women under a confinement think.

[MANLY.

I know there are whose eyes reflect more obscenity than the glasses in alcoves, but there are others too who use a little art with their looks to make 'em seem more beautiful, not more loving, which vain young fellows like you are apt to interpret in their own favour and to the lady's wrong.

FIDELIA.

Seldom, sir. Pray have you a care of gloating eyes, for he that loves to gaze upon 'em will find at last a thousand fools and cuckolds in 'em, instead of cupids.]

MANLY.

Very well, sir. But, what, you had only eye-kindness from Olivia?

FIDELIA.

I tell you again, sir, no woman sticks there. [Eye-promises of love they only keep; nay, they are contracts which make you sure of 'em. In short, sir,] she, seeing me with shame and amazement dumb, unactive and resistless, threw her twisting arms about my neck and smothered me with a thousand tasteless kisses – believe me, sir, they were so to me.

MANLY.

Why did you not avoid 'em then?

FIDELIA.

I fenced with her eager arms as you did with the grapples of

the enemy's fireship and nothing but cutting 'em off could
have freed me.

MANLY.

Damned, damned woman, that could be so false and
infamous! And damned, damned heart of mine, that cannot
yet be false, though so infamous! What easy, tame, suffering,
trampled things does that little god of talking cowards make
of us! But –

FIDELIA (*aside*).

So! It works I find as I expected.

MANLY.

But she was false to me before. She told me so herself, and yet
I could not quite believe it. But she was, so that her second
falseness is a favour to me, not an injury, in revenging me
upon the man that wronged me first of her love. Her love! – A
whore's, a witch's love! – But, what, did she not kiss well, sir?
I'm sure I thought her lips – but I must not think of 'em more
– but yet they are such I could still kiss – grow to – and then
tear off with my teeth, grind 'em into mammocks and spit 'em
into her cuckold's face.

FIDELIA (*aside*).

Poor man, how uneasy he is! I have hardly the heart to give
him so much pain, though withal I give him a cure and to
myself new life.

MANLY.

But, what, her kisses sure could not but warm you into desire
at last or a compliance with hers at least?

FIDELIA.

Nay, more, I confess –

MANLY.

What more? Speak.

FIDELIA.

All you could fear had passed between us, if I could have been
made to wrong you, sir, in that nature.

MANLY.

Could have been made! You lie, you did.

FIDELIA.

Indeed, sir, 'twas impossible for me; besides, we were
interrupted by a visit. But, I confess, she would not let me stir
till I promised to return to her again within this hour, as soon
as it should be dark, by which time she would dispose of her
visit and her servants and herself for my reception, which I
was fain to promise to get from her.

MANLY.

Ha!

FIDELIA.

But if ever I go near her again, may you, sir, think me as fals
to you as she is, hate and renounce me, as you ought to do he
and I hope will do now.

MANLY.

Well, but now I think on't, you shall keep your word wit
your lady. What, a young fellow and fail the first, nay, s
tempting an assignation!

FIDELIA.

How, sir?

MANLY.

I say you shall go to her when 'tis dark and shall not dis
appoint her.

FIDELIA.

I, sir! I should disappoint her more by going, for –

MANLY.

How so?

FIDELIA.

Her impudence and injustice to you will make me disappoin
her love, loathe her.

MANLY.

Come, you have my leave and, if you disgust her, I'll go wit
you and act love whilst you shall talk it only.

FIDELIA.

You, sir! Nay, then I'll never go near her. You act love, sir
You must but act it indeed after all I have said to you. Thin
of your honour, sir. Love –

MANLY.

Well, call it revenge and that is honourable. I'll be revenge
on her and thou shalt be my second.

FIDELIA.

Not in a base action, sir, when you are your own enemy. O, g
not near her, sir, for heaven's sake, for your own, think not o
it.

MANLY.

How concerned you are! I thought I should catch you. What
you are my rival at last and are in love with her yourself an
have spoken ill of her out of your love to her, not me, an
therefore would not have me go to her!

FIDELIA.

Heaven witness for me, 'tis because I love you only I would not have you go to her.

MANLY.

Come, come, the more I think on't, the more I'm satisfied you do love her. Those kisses, young man, I knew were irresistible; 'tis certain.

FIDELIA.

There is nothing certain in the world, sir, but my truth and your courage.

MANLY.

Your servant, sir. Besides, false and ungrateful as she has been to me, and though I may believe her hatred to me as great as you report it, yet I cannot think you are so soon and at that rate beloved by her, though you may endeavour it.

FIDELIA.

Nay, if that be all and you doubt it still, sir, I will conduct you to her and, unseen, your ears shall judge of her falseness and my truth to you, if that will satisfy you.

MANLY.

Yes, there is some satisfaction in being quite out of doubt: because 'tis that alone withholds us from the pleasure of revenge.

FIDELIA.

Revenge! What revenge can you have, sir? Disdain is best revenged by scorn, and faithless love by loving another and making her happy with the other's losings, which, if I might advise –

Enter Freeman.

MANLY.

Not a word more.

FREEMAN.

What, are you talking of love yet, captain? I thought you had done with't.

MANLY.

Why, what did you hear me say?

FREEMAN.

Something imperfectly of love, I think.

MANLY.

I was only wondering why fools, rascals and desertless wretches should still have the better of men of merit with all women, as much as with their own common mistress, Fortune!

FREEMAN.

Because most women, like Fortune, are blind, seem to do all things in jest and take pleasure in extravagant actions. Their love deserves neither thanks or blame, for they cannot help it; 'tis all sympathy. Therefore the noisy, the finical, the talkative, the cowardly and effeminate have the better of the brave, the reasonable and man of honour, for they have no more reason in their love or kindness than Fortune herself.

MANLY.

Yes, they have their reason. First, honour in a man they fear too much to love and sense in a lover upbraids their want of it and they hate anything that disturbs their admiration of themselves; but they are of that vain number who had rather show their false generosity in giving away profusely to worthless flatterers than in paying just debts. And, in short, all women, like Fortune, as you say, and rewards, are lost by too much meriting.

FIDELIA.

All women, sir! Sure, there are some who have no other quarrel to a lover's merit but that it begets their despair of him.

MANLY.

Thou art young enough to be credulous, but we –

Enter First Sailor.

FIRST SAILOR

Here are now below the scolding, daggled gentlewoman and that Major Old – old – Fop, I think you call him.

FREEMAN.

Oldfox. Prithee, bid 'em come up, with your leave, captain, for now I can talk with her upon the square, if I shall not disturb you.

MANLY.

No, for I'll be gone. Come, volunteer.

FREEMAN.

Nay, pray stay. The scene between us will not be so tedious to you as you think. Besides, you shall see how I have rigged my squire out with the remains of my shipwrecked wardrobe. He is under your sea *valet de chambre*'s hands and by this time dressed and will be worth your seeing. Stay and I'll fetch my fool.

MANLY.

No, you know I cannot easily laugh; besides, my volunteer and I have business abroad.

Exeunt Manly, Fidelia, on one side, Freeman on t'other. Enter Major Oldfox and Widow Blackacre.

WIDOW.

What, nobody here! Did not the fellow say he was within?

OLDFOX.

Yes, lady, and he may be perhaps a little busy at present, but if you think the time long till he comes, (*unfolding papers*). I'll read you here some of the fruits of my leisure, the overflowings of my fancy and pen. (*Aside.*) To value me right, she must know my parts. – Come –

WIDOW.

No, no, I have reading work enough of my own in my bag, I thank you.

OLDFOX.

Ay, law, madam, but here is a poem in blank verse which I think a handsome declaration of one's passion.

WIDOW.

O! If you talk of declarations, I'll show you one of the prettiest penned things which I mended too myself you must know.

OLDFOX.

Nay, lady, if you have used yourself so much to the reading of harsh law that you hate smooth poetry, here is a character for you of –

WIDOW.

A character! Nay, then I'll show you my bill in Chancery here that gives you such a character of my adversary, makes him as black –

OLDFOX.

Pshaw, away, away, lady. But if you think the character too long, here is an epigram not above twenty lines, upon a cruel lady who decreed her servant should hang himself to demonstrate his passion.

WIDOW.

Decreed! If you talk of decreeing, I have such a decree here, drawn by the finest clerk –

OLDFOX.

O lady, lady, all interruption and no sense between us, as if we were lawyers at the bar! [But I had forgot, Apollo and Littleton never lodge in a head together.] If you hate verses, I'll give you a cast of my politics in prose: 'tis a letter to a friend in the country, which is now the way of all such sober solid persons as myself, when they have a mind to publish their disgust to the times, though perhaps, between you and I, they have no friend in the country. And, sure, a politic serious person may as well have a feigned friend in the country to write to as well as an idle poet a feigned mistress to write to. And so here is my letter to a friend, or no friend, in the country concerning the late conjuncture of affairs in relation to coffeehouses, or the Coffeeman's Case.

WIDOW.

Nay, if your letter have a case in't, 'tis something, but first I'll read you a letter of mine [to a friend in the country,] called a letter of attorney.

Enter to them Freeman and Jerry Blackacre in a gaudy suit and red breeches of Freeman's.

OLDFOX (*aside*).

What, interruption still? O the plague of interruption, [worse to an author than the plague of critics!]

WIDOW.

What's this I see, Jerry Blackacre, my minor, in red breeches! What, hast thou left the modest, seemly garb of gown and cap for this? And have I lost all my good Inns of Chancery breeding upon thee then? And thou wilt go a-breeding thyself [from our Inn of Chancery and Westminster Hall,] at coffeehouses and ordinaries, playhouses, tennis courts and bawdyhouses.

JERRY.

Ay, ay, what then? Perhaps I will. But what's that to you? Here's my guardian and tutor now, forsooth, that I am out of your huckster's hands.

WIDOW.

How? Thou hast not chosen him for thy guardian yet?

JERRY.

No, but he has chosen me for his charge and that's all one, and I'll do anything he'll have me and go all the world over with him, to ordinaries and bawdyhouses, or anywhere else.

WIDOW.

To ordinaries and bawdyhouses! Have a care, minor. Thou wilt infeeble there thy estate and body. Do not go to ordinaries and bawdyhouses, good Jerry.

JERRY.

Why, how come you to know any ill by bawdyhouses? You never had any hurt by 'em, had you, forsooth? Pray hold yourself contented. If I do go where money and wenches are to be had, you may thank yourself, for you used me so unnaturally, you would never let me have a penny to go abroad with nor so much as come near the garret where your maidens lay; nay, you would not so much as let me play at hotcockles with 'em nor have any recreation with 'em, though one should have kissed you behind, you were so unnatural a mother, so you were.

FREEMAN.

Ay, a very unnatural mother, faith, squire.

WIDOW.

But Jerry, consider thou art yet but a minor. However, if thou wilt go home with me again and be a good child, thou shalt see –

FREEMAN.

Madam, I must have a better care of my heir under age than so. I would sooner trust him alone with a stale waiting-woman and a parson than with his widow-mother and her lover or lawyer.

WIDOW.

Why, thou villain, part mother and minor! Rob me of my child and my writings! But thou shalt find there's law, and as in the case of ravishment of guard – Westminster the second.

OLDFOX.

Young gentleman, squire, pray be ruled by your mother and your friends.

JERRY.

Yes, I'll be ruled by my friends, therefore not by my mother, so I won't. I'll choose him for my guardian till I am of age, nay, maybe for as long as I live.

WIDOW.

Wilt thou so, thou wretch? And when thou'rt of age, thou wilt sign, seal and deliver too, wilt thou?

JERRY.

Yes, marry will I, if you go there too.

WIDOW.

O do not squeeze wax, son. Rather go to ordinaries and bawdyhouses than squeeze wax. If thou dost that, farewell the goodly manor of Blackacre with all its woods, underwoods and appurtenances whatever. Oh, oh! (*Weeps*.)

FREEMAN.

Come, madam, in short, you see I am resolved to have a share in the estate, yours or your son's: if I cannot get you, I'll keep

him, who is less coy you find; but if you would have your son again, you must take me too. Peace or war? Love or law? You see my hostage is in my hand. I'm in possession.

WIDOW.

Nay, if one of us must be ruined, e'en let it be him. By my body, a good one! Did you ever know yet a widow marry or not marry for the sake of her child? I'd have you to know, sir, I shall be hard enough for you both yet without marrying you, if Jerry won't be ruled by me. What say you, booby, will you be ruled? Speak.

JERRY.

Let one alone, can't you?

WIDOW.

Wilt thou choose him for guardian whom I refuse for husband?

JERRY.

Ay, to choose, I thank you.

WIDOW.

And are all my hopes frustrated? Shall I never hear thee put cases again to John the butler or our vicar? Never see thee amble the circuit with the judges and hear thee in our town hall louder than the crier?

JERRY.

No, for I have taken leave of lawyering and pettifogging.

WIDOW.

Pettifogging! Thou profane villain, hast thou so? Pettifogging! – Then you shall take your leave of me and your estate too. Thou shalt be an alien to me and it forever. Pettifogging!

JERRY.

O, but if you go there too, mother, we have the deeds and settlements, I thank you. Would you cheat me of my estate, ifac?

WIDOW.

No, no, I will not cheat your little brother Bob, for thou wert not born in wedlock.

FREEMAN.

How's that?

JERRY.

How? What quirk has she got in her head now?

WIDOW.

I say thou canst not, shalt not inherit the Blackacres' estate.

JERRY.

Why? Why, forsooth? What d'ye mean, if you go there too?

WIDOW.

Thou art but my base child and according to the law canst not inherit it; nay, thou art not so much as bastard eigne.

JERRY.

What, what? Am I then the son of a whore, mother?

WIDOW.

The law says –

FREEMAN.

Madam, we know what the law says, but have a care what you say. Do not let your passion to ruin your son ruin your reputation.

WIDOW.

Hang reputation, sir. Am not I a widow? Have no husband nor intend to have any? Nor would you, I suppose, now have me for a wife. So I think now I'm revenged on my son and you, without marrying, as I told you.

FREEMAN.

But consider, madam.

JERRY.

What, have you no shame left in you, mother?

WIDOW (aside to Oldfox).

Wonder not at it, major. 'Tis often the poor pressed widow's case, to give up her honour to save her jointure and seem to be a light woman rather than marry, [as some young men, they say, pretend to have the filthy disease and lose their credit with most women to avoid the importunities of some.]

FREEMAN.

But one word with you, madam.

WIDOW.

No, no, sir. Come, major, let us make haste now to the Prerogative Court.

OLDFOX.

But, lady, if what you say be true, will you stigmatise your reputation on record? And, if it be not true, how will you prove it?

WIDOW.

Pshaw! I can prove anything and, for my reputation, know, major, a wise woman will no more value her reputation in disinheriting a rebellious son of a good estate than she would in

getting him to inherit an estate.

Exeunt Widow and Oldfo[x]

FREEMAN.

Madam – We must not let her go so, squire.

JERRY.

Nay, the devil can't stop her though if she has a mind to't. B[ut] come, bully guardian, we'll go and advise with three attornie[s] two proctors, two solicitors and a shrewd man of Whitefriar[s] neither attorney, proctor or solicitor but as pure a pimp to th[e] law as any of 'em; and, sure, all they will be hard enough fo[r] her, for I fear, bully guardian, you are too good a joker to hav[e] any law in your head.

FREEMAN.

Thou'rt in the right on't, squire; I understand no law especially that against bastards, since I'm sure [the custom i[s] against that law, and] more people get estates by being so tha[n] lose 'em.

Exeun[t]

Scene Two

The scene changes to Olivia's lodgings. Enter Lord Plausible and Bo[y] with a candle

LORD PLAUSIBLE.

Little gentleman, your most obedient, faithful, humb[le] servant; where, I beseech you, is that divine person, yo[ur] noble lady?

BOY.

Gone out, my lord, but commanded me to give you this lette[r]. (*Gives him a letter.*)

Enter to him Novel.

LORD PLAUSIBLE (aside).

Which he must not observe. (*Puts it up.*)

NOVEL.

Hey, boy, where is thy lady?

BOY.

Gone out, sir, but I must beg a word with you.

Gives him a letter and exi[t]

NOVEL.

For me? So. (*Puts up the letter.*) Servant, servant, my lor[d] You see the lady knew of your coming, for she is gone out.

LORD PLAUSIBLE.
Sir, I humbly beseech you not to censure the lady's good breeding. She has reason to use more liberty with me than with any other man.

NOVEL.
How, viscount, how?

LORD PLAUSIBLE.
Nay, I humbly beseech you, be not in choler. Where there is most love there may be most freedom.

NOVEL.
Nay, then 'tis time to come to an éclaircissement with you and to tell you you must think no more of this lady's love.

LORD PLAUSIBLE.
Why, under correction, dear sir?

NOVEL.
There are reasons, reasons, viscount.

LORD PLAUSIBLE.
What, I beseech you, noble sir?

NOVEL.
Prithee, prithee, be not impertinent, my lord. Some of you lords are such conceited, well-assured, impertinent rogues.

LORD PLAUSIBLE.
And you noble wits are so full of shamming and drolling one knows not where to have you, seriously.

NOVEL.
Well, you shall find me in bed with this lady one of these days.

LORD PLAUSIBLE.
Nay, I beseech you, spare the lady's honour, for hers and mine will be all one shortly.

NOVEL.
Prithee, my lord, be not an ass. Dost thou think to get her from me? I have had such encouragements –

LORD PLAUSIBLE.
I have not been thought unworthy of 'em.

NOVEL.
What, not like mine! Come to an éclaircissement, as I said.

LORD PLAUSIBLE.
Why, seriously then, she has told me viscountess sounded prettily.

NOVEL.
And me that Novel was a name she would sooner change hers for than for any title in England.

LORD PLAUSIBLE.
She has commended the softness and respectfulness of my behaviour.

NOVEL.
She has praised the briskness of my raillery of all things, man.

LORD PLAUSIBLE.
The sleepiness of my eyes she liked.

NOVEL.
Sleepiness! Dullness, dullness. But the fierceness of mine she adored.

LORD PLAUSIBLE.
The brightness of my hair she liked.

NOVEL.
The brightness! No, the greasiness, I warrant. But the blackness and lustre of mine she admires.

LORD PLAUSIBLE.
The gentleness of my smile.

NOVEL.
The subtlety of my leer.

LORD PLAUSIBLE.
The clearness of my complexion.

NOVEL.
The redness of my lips.

LORD PLAUSIBLE.
The whiteness of my teeth.

NOVEL.
My janty way of picking them.

LORD PLAUSIBLE.
The sweetness of my breath.

NOVEL.
Hah, ha! – Nay then she abused you, 'tis plain, for you know what Manly said; the sweetness of your pulvillio she might mean, but for your breath! Ha, ha, ha. Your breath is such, man, that nothing but tobacco can perfume, and your complexion nothing could mend but the smallpox.

LORD PLAUSIBLE.
Well, sir, you may please to be merry, but, to put you out of

all doubt, sir, she has received some jewels from me of value.

NOVEL.
And presents from me, besides what I presented her jantily by way of ombre, of three or four hundred pound value, which, I'm sure, are the earnest pence for our love bargain.

LORD PLAUSIBLE.
Nay then, sir, with your favour and to make an end of all your hopes, look you there, sir, she has writ to me. –

NOVEL.
How! How! Well, well, and so she has to me: look you there. –

Deliver to each other their letters.

LORD PLAUSIBLE.
What's here!

NOVEL
How's this? (*Reads out.*)
My Dear Lord,
You'll excuse me for breaking my word with you since 'twas to oblige, not to offend you, for I am only gone abroad but to disappoint Novel and meet you in the drawing-room, where I expect you with as much impatience as when I used to suffer Novel's visits, the most impertinent fop that ever affected the name of a wit, therefore not capable, I hope, to give you jealousy, for, for your sake alone, you saw I renounced an old lover and will do all the world. Burn the letter but lay up the kindness of it in your heart, with your
                                        Olivia

Very fine! But pray let's see mine.

LORD PLAUSIBLE.
I understand it not but, sure, she cannot think so of me.

NOVEL (*reads the other letter*).
Humh! – Ha! – meet – for your sake – umh – quitted an old lover – world – burn – in your heart, with your
                                        Olivia
Just the same, the names only altered.

LORD PLAUSIBLE.
Surely there must be some mistake, or somebody has abused her, and us.

NOVEL.
Yes, you are abused, no doubt on't, my lord, but I'll to Whitehall and see.

LORD PLAUSIBLE.
And I, where I shall find you are abused.

NOVEL.
Where, if it be so, for our comfort we cannot fail of meetin with fellow-sufferers enough, for, as Freeman said of anothe she stands in the drawing-room like the glass, ready for comers to set their gallantry by her, and, like the glass to lets no man go from her unsatisfied with himself.
                                        Exeunt amb

Enter Olivia and Boy.

OLIVIA.
Both here and just gone?

BOY.
Yes, madam.

OLIVIA.
But are you sure neither saw you deliver the other a letter

BOY.
Yes, yes, madam, I am very sure.

OLIVIA.
Go [then to the Old Exchange, to Westminster, Holborn a all the other places I told you of; I shall not need you these tw hours. Be gone] and take the candle with you and be sure y leave word again below, I am gone out to all that ask.

BOY.
Yes, madam.
                                        Ex

OLIVIA.
And my new lover will not ask I'm sure. He has his lesson a cannot miss me here, though in the dark, which I ha purposely designed as a remedy against my blushing gallan modesty, for young lovers like gamecocks are made bolder being kept without light.

Enter her husband Vernish as from a journey.

VERNISH (*softly*).
Where is she? Darkness everywhere!

OLIVIA.
What, come before your time? My soul! My life! [Your has has augmented your kindness and let me thank you for it th and thus] – (*Embracing and kissing him.*) And though, [n soul,] the little time since you left me has seemed an age to impatience, sure it is yet but seven –

VERNISH.

How! Who's that you expected after seven?

OLIVIA (*aside*).

Ha! My husband returned! And have I been throwing away so many kind kisses on my husband and wronged my lover already?

VERNISH.

Speak, I say, who was't you expected after seven?

OLIVIA (*aside*).

What shall I say? – O – Why, 'tis but seven days, is it, dearest, since you went out of town? And I expected you not so soon.

VERNISH.

No sure, 'tis but five days since I left you.

OLIVIA.

Pardon my impatience, dearest, I thought 'em seven at least.

VERNISH.

Nay then –

OLIVIA.

But, my life, you shall never stay half so long from me again, you shan't, indeed, by this kiss, you shan't.

VERNISH.

No, no, but why alone in the dark?

OLIVIA.

Blame not my melancholy in your absence – But, my soul, since you went, I have strange news to tell you: Manly is returned.

VERNISH.

Manly returned! Fortune forbid.

OLIVIA.

Met with the Dutch in the Channel, fought, sunk his ship and all he carried with him. He was here with me yesterday.

VERNISH.

And did your own our marriage to him?

OLIVIA.

I told him I was married, to put an end to his love and my trouble, but to whom is yet a secret kept from him and all the world. And I have used him so scurvily his great spirit will ne'er return to reason it farther with me. I have sent him to sea again, I warrant.

VERNISH.

'Twas bravely done. [And sure he will now hate the shore more than ever after so great a disappointment.] Be you sure only to keep awhile our great secret till he be gone. In the meantime I'll lead the easy, honest fool by the nose as I used to do and, whilst he stays, rail with him at thee and, when he's gone, laugh with thee at him. But have you his cabinet of jewels safe? Part not with a seed pearl to him to keep him from starving.

OLIVIA.

Nor from hanging.

VERNISH.

He cannot recover 'em and, I think, will scorn to beg 'em again.

OLIVIA.

But, my life, have you taken the thousand guineas he left in my name out of the goldsmith's hands?

VERNISH.

Ay, ay, they are removed to another goldsmith's.

OLIVIA.

Ay but, my soul, you had best have a care he find not where the money is, for his present wants, [as I'm informed,] are such as will make him inquisitive enough.

VERNISH.

You say true and he knows the man too, but I'll remove it tomorrow.

OLIVIA.

Tomorrow! O do not stay till tomorrow. Go tonight, immediately.

VERNISH.

Now I think on't, you advise well and I will go presently.

OLIVIA.

Presently! Instantly! I will not let you stay a jot.

VERNISH.

I will then, though I return not home till twelve.

OLIVIA.

Nay, though not till morning with all my heart. Go, dearest, I am impatient till you are gone –

Thrusts him out.

So, I have at once now brought about those two grateful businesses which all prudent women do together, secured money and pleasure, and now all interruptions of the last are removed. Go husband and come up friend, just the buckets in the well: the absence of one brings the other but I hope, like them too, they will not meet in the way, justle and clash together.

Enter Fidelia, and Manly treading softly and staying behind at some distance.

So, are you come? (But not the husband-bucket, I hope, again.) Who's there? My dearest? (*Softly.*)

FIDELIA.
My life —

OLIVIA.
Right, right. Where are thy lips? Here, take the dumb and best welcomes, kisses and embraces; 'tis not a time for idle words. In a duel of love, [as in others] parleying shows basely. Come, we are alone, and now the word is only satisfaction and defend not thyself.

MANLY (*aside*).
How's this? Wuh, she makes love like a devil in a play [and, in this darkness, which conceals her angel's face, if I were apt to be afraid I should think her a devil.]

OLIVIA.
What, you traverse ground, young gentleman.

Fidelia avoiding her.

FIDELIA.
I take breath only.

MANLY (*aside*).
Good heavens! How was I deceived!

OLIVIA.
Nay, you are a coward. What, are you afraid of the fierceness of my love?

FIDELIA.
Yes, madam, lest its violence might presage its change and I must needs be afraid you would leave me quickly who could desert so brave a gentleman as Manly.

OLIVIA.
O! Name not his name, for in a time of stolen joys, as this, the filthy name of husband were not a more allaying sound.

MANLY (*aside*).
There's some comfort yet.

FIDELIA.
But did you not love him?

OLIVIA.
Never. How could you think it?

FIDELIA.
Because he thought it, who is a man of that sense, nic discerning and diffidency that I should think it hard t deceive him.

OLIVIA.
No, he that distrusts most the world trusts most to himsel and is but the more easily deceived because he thinks he can' be deceived. [His cunning is like the coward's sword by whic he is oftener worsted than defended.]

FIDELIA.
Yet, sure, you used no common art to deceive him.

OLIVIA.
I know he loved his own singular moroseness so well as to do upon any copy of it; wherefore I feigned an hatred to th world too that he might love me in earnest. But if it had bee hard to deceive him I'm sure 'twere much harder to love him A dogged, ill-mannered —

FIDELIA (*aside to Manly*).
D'ye hear her, sir? Pray hear her.

OLIVIA.
Surly, untractable, snarling brute! He! A masty dog were a fit a thing to make a gallant of.

MANLY (*aside*).
Ay, a goat or monkey were fitter for thee.

FIDELIA.
I must confess for my part, though my rival, I cannot but sa he has a manly handsomeness in'st face and mien.

OLIVIA.
So has a Saracen in the sign.

FIDELIA.
Is proper and well made.

OLIVIA.
As a drayman.

FIDELIA.
Has wit.

OLIVIA.
He rails at all mankind.

FIDELIA
And undoubted courage.

OLIVIA.

Like the hangman's, can murder a man when his hands are tied. He has cruelty indeed, which is no more courage than his railing is wit.

MANLY (*aside*).

[Thus women, and men like women, are too hard for us when they think we do not hear 'em and] reputation, like other mistresses, is never true to a man in his absence.

FIDELIA.

He is –

OLIVIA.

Prithee no more of him. [I thought I had satisfied you enough before that he could never be a rival for you to apprehend; and you need not be more assured of my aversion to him but by the last testimony of my love to you which I am ready to give you.] Come, my soul, this way – (*Pulls Fidelia.*)

FIDELIA.

But, madam, what could make you dissemble love to him, when 'twas so hard a thing for you, and flatter his love to you?

OLIVIA.

That which makes all the world flatter and dissemble; 'twas his money – I had a real passion for that. Yet I loved not that so well as for it to take him, for as soon as I had his money I hastened his departure like a wife who, when she has made the most of a dying husband's breath, pulls away the pillow.

MANLY (*aside*).

Damned money! Its master's potent rival still and like a saucy pimp corrupts itself the mistress it procures for us.

OLIVIA.

But I did not think with you, my life, to pass my time in talking. Come hither, come. Yet stay till I have locked a door in the other room that might chance to let us in some interruption, [which reciting poets or losing gamesters fear not more than I at this time do.]

Exit Olivia.

FIDELIA.

Well, I hope you are now satisfied, sir, and will be gone to think of your revenge.

MANLY.

No, I am not satisfied and must stay to be revenged.

FIDELIA.

How, sir? You'll use no violence to her, I hope, and forfeit your own life to take away hers? That were no revenge.

MANLY.

No, no, you need not fear; my revenge shall only be upon her honour, not her life.

FIDELIA.

How, sir? Her honour? O heavens! Consider, sir, she has no honour. D'ye call that revenge? Can you think of such a thing? But reflect, sir, how she hates and loathes you.

MANLY.

Yes, so much she hates me that it would be a revenge sufficient to make her accessory to my pleasure and then let her know it.

FIDELIA.

No, sir, no, to be revenged on her now were to disappoint her. Pray, sir, let us be gone. (*Pulls Manly.*)

MANLY.

Hold off. What, you are my rival then and therefore you shall stay and keep the door for me whilst I go in for you. But when I'm gone, if you dare to stir off from this very board [or breathe the least murmuring accent,] I'll cut her throat first [and if you love her you will not venture her life; nay, then I'll cut your throat too and I know you love your own life at least.]

FIDELIA.

But, sir, good sir.

MANLY.

Not a word more, lest I begin my revenge on her by killing you.

FIDELIA.

But are you sure 'tis revenge that makes you do this? How can it be?

MANLY.

Whist.

FIDELIA.

'Tis a strange revenge indeed.

MANLY.

If you make me stay, I shall keep my word and begin with you. No more.

Exit Manly at the same door Olivia went.

FIDELIA.

O heavens! Is there not punishment enough
In loving well, if you will have't a crime,
But you must add fresh torments daily to't
And punish us like peevish rivals still,
Because we fain would find a heaven here?
But did there never any love like me,
That, untried tortures, you must find me out?
Others, at worst, you force to kill themselves,
But I must be self-murderess of my love,
Yet will not grant me power to end my life,
My cruel life, for, when a lover's hopes
Are dead and gone, life is unmerciful. (*Sits down and weeps.*)

Enter Manly to her.

MANLY.

I have thought better on't; I must not discover myself now; I am without witnesses, for if I barely should publish it, she would deny it with as much impudence as she would act it again with this young fellow here. Where are you?

FIDELIA.

Here – oh – now I suppose we may be gone.

MANLY.

I will, but not you; you must stay and act the second part of a lover, that is, talk kindness to her.

FIDELIA.

Not I, sir.

MANLY.

No disputing, sir, you must; 'tis necessary to my design of coming again tomorrow night.

FIDELIA

What, can you come again then hither?

MANLY.

Yes, and you must make the appointment and an apology for your leaving her so soon, [for I have said not a word to her but have kept your counsel, as I expect you should do mine.] Do this faithfully and I promise you here you shall run my fortune still and we will never part as long as we live, but if you do not do it expect not to live.

FIDELIA.

'Tis hard, sir, but such a consideration will make it easier. You won't forget your promise, sir?

MANLY.

No, by heavens. But I hear her coming.

Enter Olivia to Fidelia.

OLIVIA.

Where is my life? Run from me already! You do not love m
dearest; nay, you are angry with me, for you would not s
much as speak a kind word to me within. What was th
reason?

FIDELIA.

I was transported too much.

OLIVIA.

That's kind; but come, my soul, what make you here? Let w
go in again. We may be surprised in this room, 'tis so near th
stairs.

FIDELIA.

No, we shall hear the better here if anybody should con
up.

OLIVIA.

Nay, I assure you, we shall be secure enough within. Com
come –

FIDELIA.

I am sick and, troubled with a sudden dizziness, cannot st
yet.

OLIVIA.

Come, I have spirits within.

FIDELIA.

Oh! – don't you hear a noise madam?

OLIVIA.

No, no, there is none. Come, come. (*Pulls her.*)

FIDELIA.

Indeed there is, and I love you so much I must have a care
your honour, [if you won't,] and go, but to come to yc
tomorrow night if you please.

OLIVIA.

With all my soul, but you must not go yet. Come, prithee

FIDELIA.

Oh! – I am now sicker and am afraid of one of my fits.

OLIVIA.

My fits?

FIDELIA.

Of the falling sickness, and I lie generally an hour in a trance; therefore pray consider your honour [for the sake of my love] and let me go that I may return to you often.

OLIVIA.

But you will be sure then to come tomorrow night?

FIDELIA.

Yes.

OLIVIA.

Swear.

FIDELIA.

By our past kindness.

OLIVIA.

Well go your ways then, if you will, you naughty creature you.

Exit Fidelia.

These young lovers with their fears and modesty make themselves as bad as old ones to us and I apprehend their bashfulness more than their tattling.

Fidelia returns.

FIDELIA.

O, madam, we're undone! There was a gentleman upon the stairs, coming up, with a candle, which made me retire. Look you, here he comes!

Enter Vernish and his man with a light.

OLIVIA.

How! My husband! Oh, undone indeed! This way.

Exit.

VERNISH.

Ha! You shall not scape me so, sir. (*Stops Fidelia.*)

FIDELIA (*aside*).

O heavens! More [fears, plagues and] torments yet in store!

VERNISH.

Come, sir, I guess what your business was here, but this must be your business now. Draw. (*Draws.*)

FIDELIA.

Sir –

VERNISH.

[No expostulations. I shall not care to hear of't.] Draw.

FIDELIA.

Good sir. –

VERNISH.

How, you rascal! Not courage to draw yet durst do me the greatest injury in the world? Thy cowardice shall not save thy life. (*Offers to run at Fidelia.*)

FIDELIA.

O hold, sir, and send but your servant down and I'll satisfy you, sir, I could not injure you as you imagine.

VERNISH.

Leave the light and be gone.

Exit Servant.

Now quickly, sir, [what you've to say, or –]

FIDELIA.

I am a woman, sir, a very unfortunate woman.

VERNISH.

How! A very handsome woman, I'm sure, then. Here are witnesses of't too, I confess – (*Pulls off her peruke and feels her breasts. Aside.*) Well, I'm glad to find the tables turned, my wife in more danger of cuckolding than I was.

FIDELIA.

Now, sir, I hope you are so much a man of honour as to let me go now I have satisfied you, sir.

VERNISH.

When you have satisfied me, madam, I will.

FIDELIA.

I hope, sir, you are too much of a gentleman to urge those secrets from a woman which concern her honour. You may guess my misfortune to be love by my disguise; [but a pair of breeches could not wrong you, sir.]

VERNISH.

I may believe love has changed your outside, which could not wrong me, but why did my wife run away?

FIDELIA.

I know not, sir. Perhaps because she would not be forced to discover me to you or to guide me from your suspicions that you might not discover me yourself, which ungentlemanlike curiosity I hope you will cease to have and let me go.

VERNISH.

Well, madam, if I must not know who you are, 'twill suffice for me only to know certainly what you are, which you must not deny me. Come, there is a bed within, the proper rack for lovers, and if you are a woman, there you can keep no secrets; you'll tell me there all unasked. Come. (*Pulls her.*)

FIDELIA.
Oh! What d'ye mean? Help, oh –

VERNISH.
I'll show you, but 'tis in vain to cry out. No one dares help you, for I am lord here.

FIDELIA.
Tyrant here. But if you are a master of this house, which I have taken for sanctuary, do not violate it yourself.

VERNISH.
[No, I'll preserve you here and nothing shall hurt you and will be as true to you as your disguise,] but you must trust me then. Come, come.

FIDELIA.
Oh, oh! Rather than you shall drag me to a death so horrid and so shameful I'll die here a thousand deaths; but you do not look like a ravisher, sir.

VERNISH.
Nor you like one would put me to't but if you will –

FIDELIA.
Oh! Oh! Help, help –

Enter Servant.

VERNISH.
You saucy rascal, how durst you come in when you heard a woman squeak? That should have been your cue to shut the door.

SERVANT.
I come, sir, to let you know the alderman, coming home immediately after you were at his house, has sent his cashier with the money, according to your note.

VERNISH.
Damn his money! Money never came to any, sure, unseasonably till now. Bid him stay.

SERVANT.
He says he cannot a moment.

VERNISH.
Receive it you then.

SERVANT.
He says he must have your receipt for it. He is in haste, for I hear him coming up, sir.

VERNISH.
Damn him. Help me in here then with this dishonourer of my family.

FIDELIA.
Oh! Oh!

SERVANT.
You say she is a woman, sir.

VERNISH.
No matter, sir. Must you prate?

FIDELIA.
O heavens! Is there –

They thrust her in and lock the door.

VERNISH.
Stay there, my prisoner. You have a short reprieve.
I'll fetch the gold and that she can't resist,
For with a full hand 'tis we ravish best.

Exeunt

ACT FIVE

Scene One

Eliza's lodging. Enter Olivia and Eliza.

OLIVIA.
Ah, cousin, nothing troubles me but that I have given the malicious world its revenge and reason now to talk as freely of me as I used to do of it.

ELIZA.
Faith, then, let not that trouble you, for, to be plain, cousin, the world cannot talk worse of you than it did before.

OLIVIA.
How, cousin? I'd have you to know, before this faux pas, this trip of mine, the world could not talk of me.

ELIZA.
Only that you mind other people's actions so much that you take no care of your own but to hide 'em, that, like a thief, because you know yourself most guilty you impeach your fellow criminals first to clear yourself.

OLIVIA.
O wicked world!

ELIZA.
That you pretend an aversion to all mankind in public [only that their wives and mistresses may not be jealous] and [hinder you of their conversation in private.

OLIVIA.
Base world!]

ELIZA.
That abroad you fasten quarrels upon innocent men [for talking of you,] only to bring 'em to ask you pardon at home and to become dear friends with 'em who were hardly your acquaintance before.

OLIVIA.
Abominable world!

ELIZA.
That you condemn the obscenity of modern plays only that you may not be censured for never missing the most obscene of the old ones.

OLIVIA.
Damned world!

ELIZA.
That you deface the nudities of pictures and little statues only because they are not real.

OLIVIA.
O fie, fie, fie. Hideous, hideous, cousin! The obscenity of their censures makes me blush.

ELIZA.
The truth of 'em, the naughty world would say now.

Enter Lettice hastily.

LETTICE.
O! Madam, here is that gentleman coming up who now you say is my master.

OLIVIA.
O! Cousin, whither shall I run? Protect me, or – (*Olivia runs away and stands at a distance.*)

Enter Vernish.

VERNISH.
Nay, nay, come –

OLIVIA.
O, sir, forgive me.

VERNISH.
Yes, yes, I can forgive you being alone in the dark with a woman in man's clothes, but have a care of a man in woman's clothes.

OLIVIA (*aside*).
What does he mean? He dissembles only to get me into his power. Or has my dear friend made him believe he was a woman? My husband may be deceived by him but I'm sure I was not.

VERNISH.
Come, come, you need not have lain out of your house for this, but perhaps you were afraid, when I was warm with suspicions, you must have discovered who she was; and prithee may I not know it?

OLIVIA.
She was – (*Aside.*) I hope he has been deceived, and since my lover has played the card I must not renounce.

VERNISH.
Come, what's the matter with thee? If I must not know who she is, I'm satisfied without. Come hither.

OLIVIA.
Sure you do know her. She has told you herself, I suppose.

VERNISH.
No, I might have known her better but that I was interrupted by the goldsmith, you know, and was forced to lock her into your chamber to keep her from his sight but when I returned I found she was got away by tying the window-curtains to the balcony, by which she slid down into the street, for, you must know, I jested with her and made her believe I'd ravish her, which she apprehended, it seems, in earnest.

OLIVIA.
Then she got from you?

VERNISH.
Yes.

OLIVIA.
And is quite gone?

VERNISH.
Yes.

OLIVIA.
I'm glad on't – otherwise you had ravished her, sir? But how dar'st you go so far as to make her believe you would ravish her? Let me understand that, sir. What! There's guilt in your face; you blush too – nay, then you did ravish her, you did, you base fellow. What, ravish a woman in the first month of our marriage! 'Tis a double injury to me, thou base ungrateful man. Wrong my bed already, villain! I could tear out those false eyes, barbarous, unworthy wretch.

ELIZA.
So, so! –

VERNISH.
Prithee hear, my dear.

OLIVIA.
I will never hear you, my plague, my torment.

VERNISH.
I swear – prithee hear me.

OLIVIA.
I have heard already too many of your false oaths and vows, especially your last in the church. O wicked man! And wretched woman that I was! I wish I had then sunk down into a grave rather than to have given you my hand to be led to your loathsome bed. Oh – oh – (*Seems to weep.*)

VERNISH.
So, very fine! Just a marriage quarrel! Which, though it generally begins by the wife's fault, yet in the conclusion it becomes the husband's and, whosoever offends at first, he only is sure to ask pardon at last. My dear –

OLIVIA.
My devil –

VERNISH.
Come, prithee be appeased and go home. I have bespoken our supper betimes, for I could not eat till I found you. Go, I'll give you all kind of satisfactions and one which uses to be a reconciling one, two hundred of those guineas I received last night, to do what you will with.

OLIVIA.
What, would you pay me for being your bawd?

VERNISH.
Nay, prithee no more. Go, and I'll thoroughly satisfy you when I come home, and then too we will have a fit of laughter at Manly, whom I am going to find at the Cock in Bow Street, where, I hear, he dined. Go, dearest, go home.

ELIZA (*aside*).
A very pretty turn indeed, this!

VERNISH.
Now, cousin, since by my wife I have that honour and privilege of calling you so, I have something to beg of you too, which is not to take notice of our marriage, to any whatever, yet awhile for some reasons very important to me; and next, that you will do my wife the honour to go home with her and me the favour to use that power you have with her in our reconcilement.

ELIZA.
That, I dare promise, sir, will be no hard matter. Your servant.

Exit Vernish

Well, cousin, this I confess was reasonable hypocrisy. You were the better for't.

OLIVIA.
What hypocrisy?

ELIZA.
Why, this last deceit of your husband was lawful since in your own defence.

OLIVIA.
What deceit? I'd have you to know I never deceived my husband.

ELIZA.
You do not understand me, sure. I say, this was an honest

come-off and a good one. But 'twas a sign your gallant had had enough of your conversation since he could so dextrously cheat your husband in passing for a woman!

OLIVIA.

What d'ye mean, once more, with 'my gallant' and 'passing for a woman'?

ELIZA.

What do you mean? You see your husband took him for a woman.

OLIVIA.

Whom?

ELIZA.

Hey-day! Why, the man he found you with, for whom last night you were so much afraid and who you told me –

OLIVIA.

Lord, you rave sure!

ELIZA.

Why, did not you tell me last night –

OLIVIA.

I know not what I might tell you last night, in a fright.

ELIZA.

Ay, what was that fright for? For a woman? Besides, were you not afraid to see your husband just now? I warrant, only for having been found with a woman! Nay, did you not just now too own your false step, or trip, as you called it? Which was with a woman too! Fie, this fooling is so inspid, 'tis offensive.

OLIVIA.

And fooling with my honour will be more offensive. Did you not hear my husband say he found me with a woman in man's clothes? And d'ye think he does not know a man from a woman?

ELIZA.

Not so well, I'm sure, as you do; therefore I'd rather take your word.

OLIVIA.

What, you grow scurrilous and are, I find, more censorious than the world! I must have a care of you, I see.

ELIZA.

No, you need not fear yet; I'll keep your secret.

OLIVIA.

My secret! [I'd have you to know I have no need of confidants, though you value yourself upon being a good one.

ELIZA.

O admirable confidence! You show more in denying your wickedness than other people in glorying in't.]

OLIVIA.

[Confidence, to me! To me such language!] Nay, then [I'll never see your face again.] (*Aside.*) I'll quarrel with her that people may never believe I was in her power but take for malice all the truth she may speak against me. – Lettice, where are you? Let us be gone from this censorious, ill woman.

ELIZA (*aside*).

Nay, thou shalt stay a little to damn thyself quite. – One word first, pray, madam. Can you swear that whom your husband found you with –

OLIVIA.

Swear! Ay, that whosoever 'twas that stole up, unknown, into my room when 'twas dark, I know not whether man or woman, by heavens, by all that's good or may I never more have joys here or in the other world; nay, may I eternally –

ELIZA.

Be damned, So, so, you are damned enough already by your oaths, and I enough confirmed, and now you may please to be gone. Yet take this advice with you, in this plain–dealing age, to leave off forswearing yourself; for, when people hardly think the better of a woman for her real modesty, why should you put that great constraint upon yourself to feign it?

OLIVIA.

O hideous! Hideous advice! Let us go out of the hearing of it. She will spoil us, Lettice.

Exeunt Olivia and Lettice at one door, Eliza at t'other.

Scene Two

The scene changes to the Cock in Bow Street. A table and bottles. Manly and Fidelia.

MANLY.

How! Saved her honour by making her husband believe you were a woman! 'Twas well, but hard enough to do sure.

FIDELIA.

We were interrupted before he could contradict me.

MANLY.

But can't you tell me, d'ye say, what kind of man he was?

FIDELIA.

I was so frightened, I confess, I can give no other account of him but that he was pretty tall, round-faced and one I'm sure I ne'er had seen before.

MANLY.

But she, you say, made you swear to return tonight?

FIDELIA.

But I have since sworn never to go near her again, for the husband would murder me, or worse, if he caught me again.

MANLY.

No, I'll go with you and defend you tonight and then I'll swear too never to go near her again.

FIDELIA.

Nay, indeed sir, I will not go to be accessory to your death too. Besides, what should you go again, sir, for?

MANLY.

No disputing or advice, sir. You have reason to know I am unalterable. Go therefore presently [and write her a note to inquire if her assignation with you holds and, if not to be at her own house, where else. And be importunate to gain admittance to her tonight. Let your messenger, ere he deliver your letter, inquire first if her husband be gone out. Go,] 'tis now almost six of the clock. I expect you back here before seven with leave to see her again. Go, do this dextrously and expect the performance of my last night's promise, never to part with you.

FIDELIA.

Ay, sir, but will you be sure to remember that?

MANLY.

Did I ever break my word? Go, no more replies or doubts.

Exit Fidelia.

Enter Freeman to Manly.

Where has thou been?

FREEMAN.

In the next room with my Lord Plausible and Novel.

MANLY.

Ay, we came hither because 'twas a private house, but with thee indeed no house can be private, for thou hast that pretty quality of the familiar fops of the town who in an eating-house always keep company with all people in't but those they came with.

FREEMAN.

I went into their room but to keep them and my own fool the squire out of your room; but you shall be peevish now because you have no money. But why the devil won't you write to those we were speaking of? Since your modesty or your spirit will not suffer you to speak to 'em to lend you money, why won't you try 'em at last that way?

MANLY.

Because I know 'em already and can bear want better than denials, nay, than obligations.

FREEMAN.

Deny you! They cannot. All of 'em have been your intimate friends.

MANLY.

No, they have been people only I have obliged particularly.

FREEMAN.

Very well, therefore you ought to go to 'em the rather, sure.

MANLY.

No, no. Those you have obliged most, most certainly avoid you when you can oblige 'em no longer [and they take your visits like so many duns.] Friends, like mistresses, are avoided for obligations past.

FREEMAN.

Pshaw! But most of 'em are your relations, men of great fortune and honour.

MANLY.

Yes, but relations have so much honour as to think poverty taints the blood and disown their wanting kindred, believing, I suppose, that, as riches at first makes a gentleman, the want of 'em degrades him. But, damn 'em, now I'm poor I'll anticipate their contempt and disown them.

FREEMAN.

But you have many a female acquaintance whom you have been liberal to whom may have a heart to refund to you a little if you would ask it. They are not all Olivias.

MANLY.

Damn thee! How couldst thou think of such a thing? I would as soon rob my footman of his wages. [Besides, 'twere in vain too, for a wench is like a box in an ordinary, receives all people's money easily but there's no getting, nay, shaking any out again and he that fills it is sure never to keep the key.]

FREEMAN.
Well, but noble captain, would you make me believe that you who know half the town, have so many friends and have obliged so many can't borrow fifty or an hundred pound?

MANLY.
Why, noble lieutenant, you who know all the town and call all you know friends methinks should not wonder at it, since you find ingratitude too; for how many lords' families (though descended from blacksmiths or tinkers) hast thou called great and illustrious? How many ill tables called good eating? [How many noisy coxcombs wits?] How many pert, cocking cowards stout? How many tawdry, affected rogues well-dressed? [How many perukes admired?] And how many ill verses applauded? And yet canst not borrow a shilling. Dost thou expect I, who always spoke truth, should?

FREEMAN.
Nay, now you think you have paid me; but hark you, captain, I have heard of a thing called grinning honour but never of starving honour.

MANLY.
Well, but it has been the fate of some brave men; and if they won't give me a ship again I can go starve anywhere with a musket on my shoulder.

FREEMAN.
Give you a ship! Why, you will not solicit it?

MANLY.
If I have not solicited it by my services, I know no other way.

FREEMAN.
Your servant, sir. Nay, then I'm satisfied I must solicit my widow the closer and run the desperate fortune of matrimony on shore.

Exit.

Enter, to Manly, Vernish.

MANLY.
How! – Nay, here is a friend indeed, and he that has him in his arms can know no wants. (*Embraces Vernish.*)

VERNISH.
Dear sir! And he that is in your arms is secure from all fears whatever. Nay, our nation is secure by your defeat at sea and the Dutch that fought against you have proved enemies to themselves only, in bringing you back to us.

MANLY.
Fie, fie! This from a friend? And yet from any other 'twere unsufferable. I thought I should never have taken anything ill from you.

VERNISH.
A friend's privilege is to speak his mind though it be taken ill.

MANLY.
But your tongue need not tell me you think too well of me. I have found it from your heart, which spoke in actions, your unalterable heart. But Olivia is false, my friend, which I suppose is no news to you.

VERNISH (*aside*).
He's in the right on't.

MANLY.
But couldst thou not keep her true to me?

VERNISH.
Not for my heart, sir.

MANLY.
But could you not perceive it at all before I went? Could she so deceive us both?

VERNISH.
I must confess, the first time I knew it was three days after your departure when she received the money you had left in Lombard Street in her name, and her tears did not hinder her it seems from counting that. You would trust her with all, like a true, generous lover!

MANLY.
And she, like a mean jilting–

VERNISH.
Traitorous –

MANLY.
Base –

VERNISH.
Damned –

MANLY.
Covetous –

VERNISH.
Mercenary whore – (*Aside.*) I can hardly hold from laughing.

MANLY.

Ay, a mercenary whore indeed, for she made me pay her before I lay with her.

VERNISH.

How! – Why, have you lain with her?

MANLY.

Ay, ay.

VERNISH.

Nay, she deserves you should report it at least, though you have not.

MANLY.

Report it! By heaven, 'tis true.

VERNISH.

How! Sure not.

MANLY.

I do not use to lie, nor you to doubt me.

VERNISH.

When?

MANLY.

Last night about seven or eight of the clock.

VERNISH (*aside*).

Ha! – Now I remember, I thought she spake as if she expected some other rather than me. A confounded whore indeed!

MANLY.

But, what, thou wonderest at it! Nay, you seem to be angry too.

VERNISH.

I cannot but be enraged against her for her usage of you, damned, infamous, common jade.

MANLY.

Nay, her cuckold, who first cuckolded me in my money, shall not laugh all himself. We will do him reason, shan't we?

VERNISH.

Ay, ay.

MANLY.

But thou dost not, for so great a friend, take pleasure enough in your friend's revenge, methinks.

VERNISH.

Yes, yes, I'm glad to know it since you have lain with her.

MANLY.

Thou canst not tell me who that rascal, her cuckold, is?

VERNISH.

No.

MANLY.

She would keep it from you, I suppose.

VERNISH.

Yes, yes –

MANLY.

Thou wouldst laugh if thou knewest but all the circumstances of my having her. Come, I'll tell thee.

VERNISH.

Damn her. I care not to hear any more of her.

MANLY.

Faith, thou shalt. You must know –

Enter Freeman, backwards, endeavouring to keep out Novel Lord Plausible, Jerry and Oldfox, who all press in upon him.

FREEMAN.

I tell you he has a wench with him and would be private.

MANLY.

Damn 'em! A man can't open a bottle in these eating-houses but presently you have these impudent, intruding, buzzing flies and insects in your glass. – Well, I'll tell thee all anon. In the meantime, prithee go to her, but not from me, and try if you can get her to lend me but an hundred pound of my money to supply my present wants, for I suppose there is no recovering any of it by law.

VERNISH.

Not any. Think not of it, nor by this way neither.

MANLY.

Go, try, at least.

VERNISH.

I'll go, but I can satisfy you beforehand, 'twill be to no purpose. [You'll no more find a refunding wench –]

MANLY.

[Than a refunding lawyer; indeed their fees alike scarce ever return.] However, try her, put it to her.

VERNISH.

Ay, ay, I'll try her, put it to her home, with a vengeance.

Exit Vernish

NOVEL.

Nay, you shall be our judge, Manly. Come, major, I'll speak it to your teeth. If people provoke me to say bitter things to their faces, they must take what follows, though, like my Lord Plausible, I'd rather do't civilly behind their backs.

MANLY.

Nay, thou art a dangerous rogue, I've heard, behind a man's back.

LORD PLAUSIBLE.

You wrong him sure, noble captain. He would do a man no more harm behind his back than to his face.

FREEMAN.

I am of my lord's mind.

MANLY.

Yes, a fool, like a coward, is the more to be feared behind a man's back, more than a witty man, for as a coward is more bloody than a brave man a fool is more malicious than a man of wit.

NOVEL.

A fool, tar – a fool! Nay, thou art a brave sea-judge of wit! A fool! Prithee, when did you ever find me want something to say, as you do often?

MANLY.

Nay, I confess, thou art always talking, roaring or making a noise; that I'll say for thee.

NOVEL.

Well, and is talking a sign of a fool?

MANLY.

Yes, always talking, especially too if it be loud and fast, is the sign of a fool.

NOVEL.

Pshaw! Talking is like fencing, the quicker the better; run 'em down, run 'em down, no matter for parrying, push on still, sa, sa, sa. No matter whether you argue in form, push in guard or no.

MANLY.

Or hit or no. I think thou always talkest without thinking, Novel.

NOVEL.

Ay, ay, studied play's the worse, to follow the allegory, as the old pedant says.

OLDFOX.

A young fop!

MANLY.

I ever thought the man of most wit had been like him of most money, who has no vanity in showing it everywhere, whilst the beggarly pusher of his fortune has all he has about him still, only to show.

NOVEL.

Well, sir, and makes a very pretty show in the world, let me tell you, nay, a better than your close hunks. A pox, give me ready money in play. What care I for a man's reputation? What are we the better for your substantial, thrifty curmudgeon in wit, sir?

OLDFOX.

Thou art a profuse young rogue indeed.

NOVEL.

So much for talking, which I think I have proved a mark of wit, and so is railing, roaring and making a noise, for railing is satire, you know, and roaring and making a noise, humour.

Enter to them Fidelia, taking Manly aside and showing him a paper.

FIDELIA.

The hour is betwixt seven and eight exactly. 'Tis now half an hour after six.

MANLY.

Well, go then to the Piazza and wait for me; [as soon as it is quite dark I'll be with you. I must stay here yet awhile for my friend.] But is railing satire, Novel?

Exit Fidelia.

FREEMAN.

And roaring and making a noise humour?

NOVEL.

What, won't you confess there's humour in roaring and making a noise?

FREEMAN.

No.

NOVEL.

Nor in cutting napkins and hangings?

MANLY.

No, sure.

NOVEL.

Dull fops!

OLDFOX.

O rogue, rogue, insipid rogue! Nay, gentlemen, allow him those things for wit, for his parts lie only that way.

NOVEL.

Peace, old fool, I wonder not at thee, but that young fellows should be so dull as to say there's no humour in making a noise and breaking windows! I tell you, there's wit and humour too in both. And a wit is as well known by his frolic as by his simile.

OLDFOX.

Pure rogue! There's your modern wit for you! Wit and humour in breaking of windows! There's mischief if you will but no wit or humour.

NOVEL.

Prithee, prithee peace, old fool. I tell you, where there is mischief there's wit. Don't we esteem the monkey a wit amongst beasts only because he's mischievous? And let me tell you, as good nature is a sign of a fool, being mischievous is a sign of wit.

OLDFOX.

O rogue, rogue! Pretend to be a wit by doing mischief and railing!

NOVEL.

Why, thou, old fool, hast no other pretence to the name of a wit but by railing at new plays.

OLDFOX.

Thou by railing at that facetious, noble way of wit, quibbling.

NOVEL.

Thou call'st thy dullness, gravity and thy dozing, thinking.

OLDFOX.

You, sir, your dullness, spleen. And you talk much and say nothing.

NOVEL.

Thou readest much and understand'st nothing, sir.

OLDFOX.

You laugh loud and break no jest.

NOVEL.

You rail and nobody hangs himself. And thou hast nothing of the satyr but in thy face.

OLDFOX.

And you have no jest but your face, sir.

NOVEL.

Thou art an illiterate pedant.

OLDFOX.

Thou art a fool with a bad memory.

MANLY.

Come, a pox on you both. You have done like wits now, fo you wits, when you quarrel, never give over till you prove on another fools.

NOVEL.

And you fools have never any occasion of laughing at us wit but when we quarrel; therefore let us be friends, Oldfox.

MANLY.

They are such wits as thou art who make the name of a wit a scandalous as that of a bully and signify a loud-laughing, talk ing, incorrigible coxcomb, as bully a roaring, hardene coward.

FREEMAN.

And would have his noise and laughter pass for wit, as t'othe his huffing and blustering for courage.

Enter Vernish.

MANLY.

Gentlemen, with your leave, here is one I would speak wit and I have nothing to say to you.

Pulls 'em out of the room

VERNISH.

I told you 'twas in vain to think of getting money out of he She says, if a shilling would do't, she would not save you fro starving or hanging or what you would think worse, beggin or flattering, and rails so at you one would not think you ha lain with her.

MANLY.

O friend, never trust for that matter a woman's railing, for sh is no less a dissembler in her hatred than her love. And as he fondness of her husband is a sign he's a cuckold, her railing another man is a sign she lies with him.

VERNISH (*aside*).

He's in the right on't. I know not what to trust to.

MANLY.

But you did not take any notice of it to her, I hope?

ACT FIVE, SCENE TWO   69

VERNISH (*aside*).
So! Sure he is afraid I should [have] disprove[d] him, by an inquiry of her. All may be well yet.

MANLY.
What hast thou in thy head that makes thee seem so unquiet?

VERNISH.
Only this base, impudent woman's falseness; I cannot put her out of my head.

MANLY.
O my dear friend, be not you too sensible of my wrongs, for then I shall feel 'em too, with more pain, and think 'em unsufferable. Damn her, her money and that ill-natured whore, too, Fortune herself; but if thou wouldst ease a little my present trouble prithee go borrow me somewhere else some money. I can trouble thee.

VERNISH.
You trouble me indeed, most sensibly, when you command me anything I cannot do. I have lately lost a great deal of money at play, [more than I can yet pay,] so that [not only my money but] my credit too is gone and I know not where to borrow; but could rob a church for you. (*Aside.*) Yet would rather end your wants, by cutting your throat.

MANLY.
Nay, then I doubly feel my poverty since I'm incapable of supplying thee. (*Embraces Vernish.*)

VERNISH.
But methinks she that granted you the last favour (as they call it) should not deny you anything.

NOVEL.
Hey, tarpaulin, have you done?

Novel looks in and retires again.

VERNISH.
I understand not that point of kindness, I confess.

MANLY.
No, thou dost not understand it and I have not time to let you know all now, for these fools, you see, will interrupt us; but anon, at supper, we'll laugh at leisure together at Olivia's cuckold, who took a young fellow that goes between his wife and me for a woman.

VERNISH.
Ha!

MANLY.
Senseless, easy rascal! 'Twas no wonder she chose him for a husband, but she thought him, I thank her, fitter than me for that blind, bearing office.

VERNISH (*aside*).
I could not be deceived in that long woman's hair tied up behind nor those infallible proofs, her pouting, swelling breasts; I have handled too many sure not to know 'em.

MANLY.
What, you wonder the fellow could be such a blind coxcomb!

VERNISH.
Yes, yes –

NOVEL.
Nay, prithee come to us, Manly. Gad, all the fine things one says in their company are lost without thee.

Novel looks in again and retires.

MANLY.
Away, fop, I'm busy yet. – You see we cannot talk here at our ease; besides, I must be gone immediately in order to meeting with Olivia again tonight.

VERNISH.
Tonight! It cannot be, sure –

MANLY.
I had an appointment just now from her.

VERNISH.
For what time?

MANLY.
At half an hour after seven precisely.

VERNISH.
Don't you apprehend the husband?

MANLY.
He! Snivelling gull! He a thing to be feared! A husband, the tamest of creatures!

VERNISH (*aside*).
Very fine!

MANLY.
But, prithee, in the meantime go try to get me some money. Though thou art too modest to borrow for thyself, thou canst do anything for me, I know. Go, for I must be gone to Olivia. Go and meet me here anon. – Freeman, where are you?

Exit Manly.

VERNISH.

Ay, I'll meet with you, I warrant, but it shall be at Olivia's. Sure it cannot be. She denies it so calmly and with that honest, modest assurance, it can't be true – and he does not use to lie – but belying a woman when she won't be kind is the only lie a brave man will least scruple. But then the woman in man's clothes, whom he calls a man! Well but by her breasts I know her to be a woman. – But then again his appointment from her to meet with him tonight! I am distracted more with doubt than jealousy. Well, I have no way to disabuse or revenge myself but by going home immediately, putting on a riding suit, and pretending to my wife the same business which carried me out of town last night requires me again to go post to Oxford tonight. Then, if the appointment he boasts of be true, it's sure to hold and I shall have an opportunity either of clearing her or revenging myself on both. Perhaps she is his wench of an old date and I am his cully whilst I think him mine and he has seemed to make his wench rich only that I might take her off of his hands; or if he has but lately lain with her, he must needs discover, by her, my treachery to him, which I'm sure he will revenge with my death and which I must prevent with his, if it were only but for fear of his too just reproaches, for, I must confess, I never had till now any excuse but that of interest for doing ill to him.

Exit Vernish.

Re-enter Manly and Freeman.

MANLY.

Come hither, only I say be sure you mistake not the time. You know the house exactly where Olivia lodges; 'tis just hard by.

FREEMAN.

Yes, yes.

MANLY.

Well then, bring 'em all, I say, thither, and all you know that may be then in the house, for the more witnesses I have of her infamy the greater will be my revenge. [And be sure you come straight up to her chamber without more ado. Here, take the watch. You see 'tis above a quarter past seven.] Be there in half an hour exactly.

FREEMAN.

You need not doubt my diligence or dexterity. I am an old scourer and can naturally beat up a wench's quarters that won't be civil. Shan't we break her windows too?

MANLY.

No, no. Be punctual only.

Exeunt ambo
Enter Widow Blackacre and two Knights of the Post; a Waiter with wine.

WIDOW.

Sweetheart, are you sure the door was shut close, that none of those roisters saw us come in?

WAITER.

Yes, mistress, and you shall have a privater room above instantly.

Exit Waiter

WIDOW.

You are safe enough, gentlemen, for I have been private in this house ere now upon other occasions when I was something younger. Come, gentlemen, [in short,] I leave my business to your care and fidelity and so, here's to you.

FIRST KNIGHT.

We were ungrateful rogues if we should not be honest to you, for we have had a great deal of your money.

WIDOW.

And you have done me many a good job for't, and so, here's to you again.

SECOND KNIGHT.

Why, we have been perjured but six times for you.

FIRST KNIGHT.

Forged but four deeds with your husband's last deed of gift.

SECOND KNIGHT.

And but three wills.

FIRST KNIGHT.

And counterfeited hands and seals to some six bonds. I think that's all, brother.

WIDOW.

Ay, that's all, gentlemen, and so, here's to you again.

SECOND KNIGHT.

Nay, 'twould do one's heart good to be forsworn for you. You have a conscience in your ways and pay us well.

FIRST KNIGHT.

You are in the right on't, brother; one would be damned for her with all one's heart.

[SECOND KNIGHT.
But there are rogues who make us forsworn for 'em and when we come to be paid they'll be forsworn too and not pay us our wages which they promised with oaths sufficient.

FIRST KNIGHT
Ay, a great lawyer, that shall be nameless bilked me too.

WIDOW.
That was hard, methinks, that a lawyer should use gentlemen witnesses no better.

SECOND KNIGHT.
A lawyer! D'ye wonder a lawyer should do't? I was bilked by a reverend divine that preaches twice on Sundays and prays half an hour still before dinner.]

WIDOW.
[How? A conscientious divine and not pay people for damning themselves! Sure then, for all his talking he does not believe damnation.] But come, to our business. Pray be sure to imitate exactly the flourish at the end of his name. (*Pulls out a deed or two.*)

FIRST KNIGHT.
O he's the best in England at untangling a flourish, madam.

WIDOW.
And let not the seal be a jot bigger. Observe well the dash too at the end of this name.

SECOND KNIGHT.
I warrant you, madam.

WIDOW.
Well, these and many other shifts poor widows are put to sometimes, for everybody would be riding a widow, as they say, and breaking into her jointure. They think marrying a widow an easy business, like leaping the hedge where another has gone over before; a widow is a mere gap, a gap with them.

Enter to them Major Oldfox with two waiters. The Knights of the Post huddle up the writings.

What, he here! Go then, go, my hearts, you have your instructions.

Exeunt Knights of the Post.

OLDFOX.
Come, madam, to be plain with you, I'll be fobbed off no longer. (*Aside.*) I'll bind her and gag her but she shall hear me. – Look you, friends, there's the money I promised you and now do you what you promised me. Here are my garters and here's a gag. You shall be acquainted with my parts, lady, you shall.

WIDOW.
Acquainted with your parts! A rape, a rape – What, will you ravish me?

The waiters tie her to the chair and gag her and exeunt.

OLDFOX.
Yes, lady, I will ravish you, but it shall be through the ear, lady, the ear only, with my well-penned acrostics.

Enter to them Freeman, Jerry Blackacre, three Bailiffs, a constable and his assistants, with the two Knights of the Post.

What, shall I never read my things undisturbed again?

JERRY.
O law! My mother bound hand and foot and gaping as if she rose before her time today!

FREEMAN.
What means this, Oldfox? But I'll release you from him. You shall be no man's prisoner but mine. Bailiffs, execute your writ. (*Freeman unties her.*)

OLDFOX.
Nay, then I'll be gone for fear of being bail and paying her debts without being her husband.

Exit Oldfox.

FIRST BAILIFF.
We arrest you, in the King's name at the suit of Mr Freeman, guardian to Jeremiah Blackacre, Esquire, in an action of ten thousand pounds.

WIDOW.
How! How! In a choke-bail action! What, and the pen-and-ink gentlemen taken too! Have you confessed, you rogues?

FIRST KNIGHT.
We needed not to confess, for the bailiffs dogged us hither to the very door and overheard all that you and we said.

WIDOW
Undone, undone then! No man was ever too hard for me till now. O, Jerry, child, wilt thou vex again the womb that bore thee?

JERRY.
Ay, for bearing me before wedlock, as you say. But I'll teach you to call a Blackacre a bastard, though you were never so much my mother.

WIDOW (*aside*).

Well, I'm undone. Not one trick left? No law-meush imaginable? – Cruel sir, a word with you I pray.

FREEMAN.

In vain, madam, for you have no other way to release yourself but by the bonds of matrimony.

WIDOW.

How, sir, how! That were but to sue out an *habeas corpus* for a removal from one prison to another. Matrimony!

FREEMAN.

Well, bailiffs, away with her.

WIDOW.

O stay, sir, can you be so cruel as to bring me under covert baron again and put it out of my power to sue in my own name? Matrimony, to a woman, is worse than excommunication in depriving her of the benefit of the law and I would rather be deprived of life. But hark you, sir, I am contented you should hold and enjoy my person by lease or patent but not by the spiritual patent called a licence, that is, to have the privileges of a husband without the dominion, that is, *durante beneplacito*; in consideration of which I will, out of my jointure, secure you an annuity of three hundred pounds a year and pay your debts, and that's all you younger brothers desire to marry a widow for, I'm sure.

FREEMAN.

Well, widow, if –

JERRY.

What, I hope, bully guardian, you are not making agreements without me?

FREEMAN.

No, no. First, widow, you must say no more that he is the son of a whore; have a care of that. And then he must have a settled exhibition of forty pounds a year and a nag of assizes, kept by you, but not upon the common, and have free ingress, egress and regress to and from your maids' garret.

WIDOW.

Well, I can grant all that too.

JERRY.

Ay, ay, fair words butter no cabbage; but, guardian, make her sign, sign and seal, for otherwise, if you knew her as well as I, you would not trust her word for a farthing.

FREEMAN.

I warrant thee, squire. Well, widow, since thou art so generous, I will be generous too, and if you'll secure me four hundred pounds a year but during your life and pay my debts, not above a thousand pound, I'll bate you your person to dispose of as you please.

WIDOW.

Have a care, sir, a settlement without a consideration is void in law. You must do something for't.

FREEMAN.

Prithee then, let the settlement on me be called alimony and the consideration our separation. Come, my lawyer, with writings ready drawn, is within and in haste. Come.

WIDOW.

But, what, no other kind of consideration, Mr Freeman? Well, a widow, I see, is a kind of a *sine cure*, by custom of which the unconscionable incumbent enjoys the profits without any duty but does that still elsewhere.

Exeunt omnes.

Scene Three

The scene changes to Olivia's lodging. Enter Olivia with a candle in her hand.

OLIVIA.

So, I am now prepared once more for my timorous young lover's reception; my husband is gone and go thou out too, thou next interrupter of love. (*Puts out the candle.*) Kind darkness that frees us lovers from scandal and bashfulness, from the censure of our gallants and the world. So, are you there?

Enter to Olivia, Fidelia, followed softly by Manly.

Come, my dear punctual lover, there is not such another in the world; thou hast beauty and youth to please a wife, address and wit to amuse and fool a husband; nay, thou hast all things to be wished in a lover but your fits. I hope, my dear, you won't have one tonight and, that you may not, I'll lock the door though there be no need of it but to lock out your fits, for my husband is just gone out of town again. Come, where are you? (*Goes to the door and locks it.*)

MANLY (*aside*).

Well, thou hast impudence enough to give me fits too [and make revenge itself impotent, hinder me from making thee yet more infamous, if it can be.]

OLIVIA.
Come, come, my soul, come.

FIDELIA.
Presently, my dear. We have time enough sure.

OLIVIA.
How! Time enough! True lovers can no more think they ever have time enough than love enough. You shall stay with me all night, but that is but a lover's moment. Come.

FIDELIA.
But won't you let me give you and myself the satisfaction of telling you how I abused your husband last night?

OLIVIA.
Not when you can give me and yourself too the satisfaction of abusing him again tonight. Come.

FIDELIA.
Let me but tell you how your husband –

OLIVIA.
O name not his or Manly's more loathsome name, if you love me. I forbid 'em last night, and you know I mentioned my husband but once and he came. No talking, pray; 'twas ominous to us. [You make me fancy a noise at the door already, but I'm resolved not to be interrupted.]

A noise at the door.

Where are you? Come, for rather than lose my dear expectation now, though my husband were at the door and the bloody ruffian Manly here in the room with all his awful insolence, I would give myself to this dear hand, to be led away to heavens of joy which none but thou canst give. But what's this noise at the door? So, I told you what talking would come to.

The noise at the door increases.

Ha! – O heavens, my husband's voice! – (*Olivia listens at the door.*)

MANLY (*aside*).
Freeman is come too soon.

OLIVIA.
O 'tis he! – Then here is the happiest minute lost that ever bashful boy or trifling woman fooled away! I'm undone! My husband's reconcilement too was false, as my joy, all delusion. But, come this way. Here's a back door. (*Exit and returns.*) The officious jade has locked us in instead of locking others out; but let us then escape your way, by the balcony, and, whilst you pull down the curtains, I'll fetch from my closet what next will best secure our escape. [I have left my key in the door and 'twill not suddenly be broke open.]

Exit.

A noise as it were people forcing the door.

MANLY.
Stir not, yet fear nothing.

FIDELIA.
Nothing but your life, sir.

MANLY.
We shall now know this happy man she calls husband.

Olivia re-enters.

OLIVIA.
O, where are you? What, idle with fear? Come, I'll tie the curtains if you will hold. Here, take this cabinet and purse, for it is thine if we escape.

Manly takes from her the cabinet and purse.

Therefore let us make haste.

Exit Olivia.

MANLY.
'Tis mine indeed now again and it shall never escape more from me, to you at least.

The door broken open, enter Vernish alone with a dark lanthorn and a sword, running at Manly, who draws, puts by the thrust and defends himself, whilst Fidelia runs at Vernish behind.

VERNISH (*with a low voice*).
So, there I'm right, sure –

MANLY (*softly*).
Sword and dark lanthorn, villain, are some odds, but –

VERNISH (*with a low voice*).
Odds! I'm sure I find more odds than I expected. What, has my insatiable two seconds at once? But –

Whilst they fight, Olivia re-enters, tying two curtains together.

OLIVIA.
Where are you now? – What, is he entered then and are they fighting? O do not kill one that can make no defence.

Manly throws Vernish down and disarms him.

How! But I think he has the better on't. Here's his scarf; 'tis he. So keep him down still. I hope thou hast no hurt, my dearest? (*Embraces Manly.*)

Enter to them Freeman, Lord Plausible, Novel, Jerry Blackacre and the Widow Blackacre, lighted in by the two sailors with torches.

Ha! – What? – Manly! And have I been thus concerned for him, embracing him? And has he his jewels again too? What means this? O, 'tis too sure, as well as my shame, which I'll go hide for ever!

Offers to go out; Manly stops her.

MANLY.
No, my dearest, after so much kindness as has passed between us, I cannot part with you yet. Freeman, let nobody stir out of the room, for, notwithstanding your lights, we are yet in the dark till this gentleman please to turn his face. – (*Pulls Vernish by the sleeve.*) How! Vernish! Art thou the happy man then? Thou! Thou! Speak, I say. But thy guilty silence tells me all. – Well, I shall not upbraid thee, for my wonder is striking me as dumb as thy shame has made thee. But, what? My little volunteer hurt and fainting!

FIDELIA.
My wound, sir, is but a slight one, in my arm. 'Tis only my fear of your danger, sir, not yet well over.

MANLY (*observing Fidelia's hair untied behind and without a peruke, which she lost in the scuffle*). But what's here? More strange things! What means this long woman's hair? And face, now all of it appears, too beautiful for a man? Which I still thought womanish indeed! What, you have not deceived me too, my little volunteer?

OLIVIA (*aside*).
Me she has I'm sure.

MANLY.
Speak.

Enter Eliza and Lettice.

ELIZA.
What, cousin, I am brought hither by your woman, I suppose, to be a witness of the second vindication of your honour?

OLIVIA.
Insulting is not generous. You might spare me; I have you.

ELIZA.
Have a care, cousin. You'll confess anon too much and I would not have your secrets.

MANLY (*to Fidelia*).
Come, your blushes answer me sufficiently and you have been my volunteer in love.

FIDELIA.
I must confess I needed no compulsion to follow you all the world over, which I attempted in this habit, partly out of shame to own my love to you and fear of a greater shame, your refusal of it, [for I knew of your engagement to this lady and the constancy of your nature, which nothing could have altered but herself.]

MANLY.
Dear madam, I desired you to bring me out of confusion and you have given me more. I know not what to speak to you or how to look upon you. The sense of my rough, hard and ill usage of you, though chiefly your own fault, gives me more pain now 'tis over than you had when you suffered it; and if my heart, the refusal of such a woman (*Pointing to Olivia.*), were not a sacrifice to profane your love and a greater wrong to you than ever yet I did you, I would beg of you to receive it, though you used it as she had done, for though it deserved not from her the treatment she gave it, it does from you.

FIDELIA.
Then it has had punishment sufficient from her already and needs no more from me, [and, I must confess, I would not be the only cause of making you break your last night's oath to me of never parting with me, if you do not forget or repent it.]

MANLY.
Then, take forever my heart and this with it (*Gives her the cabinet.*), for 'twas given to you before and my heart was before your due. I only beg leave to dispose of these few – Here, madam, I never yet left my wench unpaid.

Takes some of the jewels and offers 'em to Olivia. She strikes 'em down. Plausible and Novel take 'em up.

OLIVIA.
So it seems, by giving her the cabinet.

LORD PLAUSIBLE.
These pendants appertain to your most faithful, humble servant.

NOVEL.
And this locket is mine, my earnest for love, which she never paid, therefore my own again.

WIDOW.

By what law, sir, pray? Cousin Olivia, a word. What, do they make a seizure on your goods and chattels, *vi et armis*? Make your demand, I say, and bring your trover, bring your trover. I'll follow the law for you.

OLIVIA.

And I my revenge.

Exit Olivia.

MANLY (*to Vernish*).

But 'tis, my friend, in your consideration most that I would have returned part of your wife's portion, for 'twere hard to take all from thee, since thou hast paid so dear for't in being such a rascal. Yet thy wife is a fortune without a portion and thou art a man of that extraordinary merit in villainy, the world and fortune can never desert thee, though I do; therefore be not melancholy. Fare you well, sir.

Exit Vernish doggedly.

Now, madam, I beg your pardon (*Turning to Fidelia.*), for lessening the present I made you, but my heart can never be lessened. [This, I confess, was too small for you before, for you deserve the Indian world and I would now go thither out of covetousness for your sake only.]

FIDELIA.

Your heart, sir, is a present of that value I can never make any return to't. (*Pulling Manly from the company.*) But I can give you back such a present as this, which I got by the loss of my father, a gentleman [of the North,] of no mean extraction, who[se only child I was, therefore] left me in the present possession of two thousand pounds a year, which I left, [with multitudes of pretenders,] to follow you, sir, [having in several public places seen you and observed your actions throughly, with admiration, when you were too much in love to take notice of mine, which yet was but too visible.] The name of my family is Grey, my other Fidelia. The rest of my story you shall know when I have fewer auditors.

MANLY.

Nay, [now,] madam, you have taken from me all power [of making you any compliment on my part,] for I was going to tell you that for your sake only I would quit the unknown pleasure of a retirement and stay in this ill world of ours still, though odious to me, [than give you more frights again at sea and make again too great a venture there in you alone.] But if I should tell you now all this [and that your virtue (since greater than I thought any was in the world) had now

reconciled me to't,] my friend here would say, 'tis your estate that has made me friends with the world.

FREEMAN.

I must confess I should, for I think most of our quarrels to the world are just such as we have to a handsome woman, only because we cannot enjoy her as we would do.

MANLY.

Nay, if thou art a plain dealer too, give me thy hand, for now I'll say I am thy friend indeed. And, for your two sakes, though I have been so lately deceived in friends of both sexes,
I will believe there are now in the world
Good-natured friends who are not prostitutes,
And handsome women worthy to be friends.
Yet for my sake let no one e'er confide
In tears or oaths, in love or friend untried.

Exeunt omnes.

[EPILOGUE

WIDOW.

To you, the judges learned in stage laws,
Our poet now, by me, submits his cause,
For with young judges, such as most of you,
The men by women best their business do;
And, truth on't is, if you did not sit here,
To keep for us a term throughout the year,
We could not live by'r tongues; nay, but for you,
Our chamber-practice would be little too.
And 'tis not only the stage practiser
Who, by your meeting, gets her living here,
For, as in Hall of Westminster,
Sleek sempstress vents, amidst the courts, her ware,
So, while we bawl, and you in judgement sit,
The visor-mask sells linen too i'th'pit.
O many of your friends, besides us here,
Do live by putting off their several ware.
Here's daily done the great affair o'th'nation;
Let love, and us then, ne'er have long vacation.
But hold; like other pleaders, I have done
Not my poor client's business, but my own.
Spare me a word then, now, for him. First know,
Squires of the long robe, he does humbly show
He has a just right in abusing you
Because he is a brother Templar too,
For, at the bar, you rally one another,
And fool, and knave, is swallowed from a brother;
If not the poet here, the Templar spare;
And maul him, when you catch him at the bar.
From you, our common modish censurers,
Your favour, not your judgement, 'tis he fears;
Of all love begs you then to rail, find fault,
For plays, like women, by the world are thought
(When you speak kindly of 'em) very naught.]